Introducing Desktop Prepress

By Tim Meehan

A Subsidiary of
Henry Holt and Co., Inc.

First Edition—1995

Printed in the United States of America.

Catalog-In-Publication Data

Meehan, Tim,
    Introducing desktop prepress / by Tim Meehan.—1st ed.
        p.   cm.
    Includes index.
    ISBN 1-55828-364-1
    1. Desktop publishing. 2. Color-printing—Data processing.
    I. Title.
    Z253.53.M44   1995
    686.2'2544536—dc20   94-47609
                                                                        CIP

10 9 8 7 6 5 4 3 2 1

MIS:Press books are available at special discounts for bulk purchases for sales promotions, premiums, fund-raising, or educational use. Special editions or book excerpts can also be created to specification.

For details contact: Special Sales Director
                            MIS:Press
                            a subsidiary of Henry Holt and Company, Inc.
                            115 West 18th Street
                            New York, New York 10011

Editor-in-Chief: *Paul Farrell*

Managing Editor: *Cary Sullivan*   Assoc. Production Editor: *Erika Putre*
Development Editor: *Michael Sprague*   Technical Editor: *Megan Pugh*
Production Editor: *Anne Alessi*   Copy Editor: *Melissa Burns*

Acknowledgements

This is the part of every good book where the author gets to publicly thank all the people and organizations that were so helpful in contributing to the success of another writing and publishing effort. A project this size would certainly be impossible without the qualified and patient help and support of so many talented people.

Creating a list of all of the people who helped by contributing their time and knowledge to this project would certainly add significantly to the page count of the book, so brevity and sincerity will have to do in place of thoroughness.

Big thanks go to the real dynamos driving this technology and the benefits we all enjoy. The people at Apple for continuing to provide us with breakthrough hardware and operating system technology. The software geniuses creating the tools we use on our machines; Tim Gill and all the people at Quark, Inc., as well as everyone at the Adobe Corporation.

Locally, there were some big guns in the pre-press service bureau and printing world who provided real-world experience and insights to the problems, partnerships and rewards of service bureau operations. Thanks to Image Systems, true designer's partners who exemplify the concept of 'service' in service bureau. At National Teleprinting, there are guys who roll up their sleeves and actually have real printer's ink under their fingernails. Thanks to some serious printing talent at Frederic Printing, who shared knowledge, insight and experience on getting ink onto paper in the real world. Thanks also to all the respondents who replied electronically to a rather lengthy survey about their real worlds. You know who you are.

Thanks to Mike Spalding of the almost-world-famous Software Development Group who was there night and day with invaluable HyperTalk scripting advice. The stacks you find on this CD contain a portion of our very souls in them.

Thanks to Michael Sprague, the best development editor in western civilization. It's a gratifying to work with a genuine professional.

Thanks to Alice I. Price, an angel in agent's clothing. None of this, not any part, not a single word would surely have made it to the printed page without her persistent help and support.

For me, the real motivation behind creating a book like this continues to be the desire to bring useful information about the best software, helpful techniques, tips and hints—to the people who will benefit the most from them; the graphic designers, illustrators and production artists who have to make great art print every day. This book is a wonderfully satisfying effort to share some helpful knowledge and maybe make a few lives a little easier along the way.

Finally, thanks to my family, friends and clients who were so patient with my lagging telephone response times while I worked on this project. I have the best family on the planet, a great puppy named Ray, and some excellent friends who are trying hard to understand why someone would spend every waking moment in front of a computer. And if it weren't for the great guys in the RMHGA and the wonderfully distracting sport of paragliding, I would surely be questioning my own sanity by now. (Of course, the same people wondering about borderline obsessive extended computer use have expressed some serious doubts about paragliding as a pastime as well.)

Thank you all!

This book was created edited composed proofed and output on a variety of Apple hardware; including Macintosh Centris 660AV, Macintosh PowerBook 170, Macintosh Quadra 950, a Power Macintosh 6100/60, printed and proofed to a variety of laser printers and color proofing devices on its way to the final output.

❊ TABLE OF CONTENTS ❊

Introduction

Welcome to the exciting world of desktop prepress production! This book will introduce you to the concepts and practices of computer-aided desktop graphics production, explaining hardware, software, and conventional business practices that you'll need to know to make the most of your experience.

This book addresses all skill levels, from the beginner all the way to the experienced professional. You'll find information here that will save time and money, make you more productive, and increase your knowledge base.

Productivity is the consistent emphasis throughout this book—how to make your time more productive as well as how your computer can help you achieve this goal. Productivity is the key issue affecting your bottom line in the world of computer graphics production. Productivity isn't measured in bits, bytes, speed, or feeds. It's a function of how efficiently your time and your system's resources are put to work.

Tips, tricks, special effects, and similar anecdotal wisdom will be presented as you progress through this book. Presented in simple terms with illustrations and sidebars, it enables you to go through the material at your own speed, getting as much as you need from the text—as you need it.

Handy tips and tricks are indicated in the sidebars by an icon like this:

TIP

Each chapter or section begins and ends with a summary of the salient points presented, making it easy to glide through the material and pick up useful information as you need it.

There's a lot here for everybody. The real focus of this effort is to save you time, money, and most importantly, headaches. Accomplishing any or all of these objectives will more than recover the cost of this book for you.

Of course, recognizing the broad spectrum of users in this industry today, one must realize that no book can be all things to all readers. However, every effort was made to create a volume of knowledge that will address common interests from which all readers in this diverse market can benefit in one way or another.

Here's a brief outline of what you will encounter in this book:

* The Introduction explains how to get the most out of this book. You're already reading it.

* Chapter One introduces you to the concept of prepress production, pros and cons, and technological advances in the field.

* Chapter Two describes the basic concept of the PostScript page description language.

* Chapter Three explains process color, introduces you to the terms and concepts of mechanical prepress color separation, compares and demonstrates the differences between conventional and digital color production methods, explains how to take full advantage of your system's capabilities, and defines the terms that are necessary to communicate with service bureaus and printers.

* Chapter Four describes all the hardware pieces and parts as well as diagrams and roadmaps of the system, including possible workstation configurations and network topologies.

* Chapter Five describes the major software products and their capabilities.

* Chapter Six suggests a method for selecting your service bureau.

* Chapter Seven describes a step-by-step checklist for making sure a job is ready to print.

* Chapter Eight is a handy guide outlining some common problems and their solutions.

* Chapter Nine discusses the legal issues of who is responsible for errors at each stage of production and emphasizes the avoidance of problems through planning and preparation.

* Chapter Ten gives real-life stories and humorous anecdotes about "projects from Hell" that produced "unexpected results" or "undocumented features."

Take it from someone who has been working to keep the ink in its place on the paper for more than 15 years, someone who's seen the art of production progress from X-acto knives, rubylith, and wax to the complex and comprehensive tools we see on our desktops today. There are some genuine and tangible benefits to working with computers to create camera-ready production art. They offer unprecedented precision and versatility, but the real benefit is speed and efficiency. Now you can make last-minute changes quickly, easily, and much more cost-efficiently than ever before.

Capabilities that were once the exclusive domain of specialized out-of-house service providers are now available right on your own desktop. Control over your work that used to belong to these outside service providers is now in your own hands. Be aware, however, that with all this new capability, you are also the steward of new responsibility.

Remember this—and be sure to proof your work as often as possible in the production process.

Chapter 1

Just What Is the Prepress Business Anyway?

* What is prepress?
* Conventional versus digital production methods
* The prepress process

What Exactly is Prepress Graphic Production?

Prepress production is the art and science of preparing typography, graphic design, illustration, and photography for printing. It is all the preparation done to precisely apply ink onto paper to create a magazine, annual report, corporate capabilities brochure, newspaper ad, newsletter, T-shirt design, or poster. In short, anything that is to be printed must be composed and prepared in a way that assures that all the ink ends up where it's supposed to be, in the correct manner.

The Printing Process Explained

The basic offset printing process has remained almost unchanged for the past 50 years or so. Ink ends up on paper in pretty much the same way all over the world. In a typical offset press, flexible aluminum plates, which are wrapped around rotating drums, pick up ink from a reservoir-and-roller system and deposit it onto paper as the paper passes between the plates and rollers. Commercial printing presses can be as simple as a one-color, single-roller, drum-and-reservoir system or as complex as six- or even eight-color assemblies that can take up as much space as a railroad car (see Figure 1.1).

FIGURE 1.1 A six-color printing press.

The entire process in its basic form is relatively simple to understand. Variations in the basic process are what allow us to produce special effects and alternative printing methods to achieve greater cost-efficiency. You can learn more about the printing process from local trade organizations, community colleges and trade schools, and technical trade magazines and publications. Following are the basic concepts and steps for production in terms that are relevant to the world of computer graphics.

Getting the ink onto the paper occurs fairly late in the printing process. The steps taking place up to that point are what determine how good the design will appear in your final product. We'll outline a simple printing procedure to explain the basic steps, but we'll look at the steps in reverse order to get a sense of how each step is interdependent with the next. So, starting from the very end of the printing line, we have the following steps.

The Last Step Before Delivery

After the actual printing (ink on paper) process is finished, and before the job is delivered to the client, it must be trimmed, scored, folded, and packaged. This is worthy of mention because the software that you used to create the camera-ready negatives for this job has already placed accurate registration marks and trim guides to indicate where the paper will trim in the final step of production (see Figure 1.2).

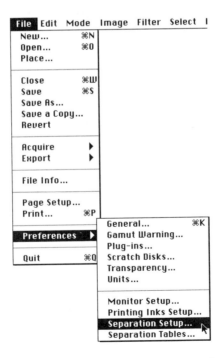

FIGURE 1.2 Don't forget to set your separations!

Most software automatically creates accurate and precise registration marks and trim lines to aid printing production.

Putting the Ink Onto the Paper

As a sheet of paper travels through the press, it passes between rollers that bring it into contact with a large cylinder around which is wrapped a flexible aluminum sheet, called a *plate*. This plate picks up ink from a system of smaller rollers that transfer ink from a reservoir to the plate (see Figure 1.3).

FIGURE 1.3 A very simplified look at how the modern printing press works.

A commercial offset press will commonly have several of these roller and plate assemblies in line, allowing the application of several colors of ink to the paper on a single pass through the press. Presses are generically referred to by the number of colors that may be applied per pass through the press. For example, a *two-color press* is able to apply two separate colors, and a *four-color press* is able to apply four colors, in a single pass. Presses are also referred to by the maximum page size that the press can accommodate. For example, a 48-inch two-color press is capable of printing two colors in a single pass onto a sheet of paper up to 48 inches wide.

Some printing establishments operate presses that can apply four, six or even eight colors in a single pass (see Figure 1.4). These presses can be as large as railroad cars and require several technicians to operate them, but they offer the advantage of being able to apply four process colors (to simulate full-color photography) as well as a combination of custom colors, including special coatings or varnishes for special effects, all at speeds of several hundred pages per minute.

FIGURE 1.4 Another view of the 6-color press.

Naturally, precision is a primary concern with so much going on so quickly. Imagine how finely tuned this large machine must be as a large sheet of paper travels through the press, acquiring several layers of ink, with each layer being placed precisely within a rigid confine of less than a thousandth of an inch.

Misregistration, or misalignment, can occur for several reasons: Paper may shift, machinery can come out of alignment, ink may spread, or paper may stretch, even a tiny amount. These occurrences will turn an accurate printing effort into second-rate work. Luckily, your software can accommodate these problems by creating tiny overlaps of color areas called *traps* to compensate for slight misalignment of colors (see Figure 1.5).

FIGURE 1.5 Mis-registered print job.

Your software can automatically create traps, bleeds, and spreads to compensate for slight misregistration on the press.

The Prepress Process

Proofs and Plates

Before the plates can be inked and ink transferred to paper, the plates must be made by exposing a light-sensitive coating. You can do this by using negatives that you create with your computer system and your high-resolution printer. Now we're getting closer to the parts that involve us, the digital artists.

Separate negatives for each necessary color or ink treatment used in your job are used as a mask to expose a photosensitive coating on the actual printing plate (see Figure 1.6). Unexposed areas on the plate resist ink and the exposed areas attract ink, which is then deposited onto the paper when it travels through the press.

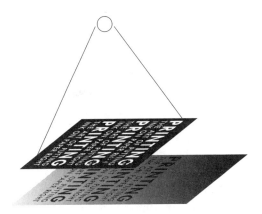

FIGURE 1.6 A negative creating a printing plate.

Negatives are composed from separations into four basic component process colors of all the colors in your printed piece: cyan (blue), magenta, yellow, and black, plus any additional special effects such as spot varnish or custom-ink colors. In conventional graphic production (before everyone on the planet was using computers to perform these functions), the separation process required complex and tedious composition services called *stripping*, in which a staff of technicians worked in a dimly lit environment, photographically composing each layer of negative film so that they registered (or aligned) correctly to produce accurate and precise proofs.

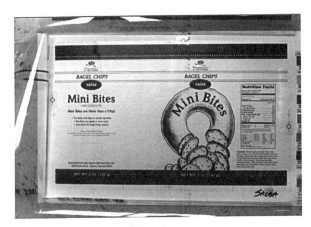

FIGURE 1.7 Conventional paste-up board.

Using these negatives, a final proof of your work is created to make sure that all the negatives have aligned correctly and that all the colors match what you had envisioned. You would likely approve a *blue-line* proof that showed your production in a single color (usually blue, hence the name) to make sure all the items were correctly positioned. You would also approve a series of color proofs made from your negatives called *match prints*, *Chromalins*, or *color keys* to make sure all separations and colors matched up correctly.

Using the final production negatives to create these proofs gives us the last, best look at the project before committing to an expensive and hard-to-interrupt printing process on a complicated machine (the press), which costs hundreds, even thousands of dollars per hour to operate.

Conventionally, these negatives are created using a labor-intensive, time-consuming, photo-mechanical process. This process involves the use of special environments and chemistry to expose film negatives shot with huge floor-standing cameras onto large-format film (see Figure 1.8). Negatives must be carefully tested throughout the process to insure proper dot densities, calibration, and registration. True craftsmen are at work in this department to determine the proper construction and composition of negatives to achieve the results you desire.

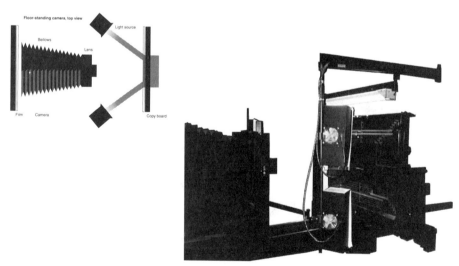

FIGURE 1.8 The cameras used to create printing film.

With a computer system, your page-layout software automatically composes and separates all the negatives, drastically reducing the amount of stripping and composition services required in a conventional production method.

Most of the graphic production software you're using with your computer system will automatically generate accurate color separations onto separate negatives, including full-color photographs and matched-process color elements. This will significantly reduce the amount of time and intervention necessary in the stripping department of your print shop.

Proofs and Negatives

Before your final negatives are produced on your high-resolution printer, you'll want to proof your work using some kind of color-proofing system. This provides a semi-accurate indication of where all the colors, photography, and type will fall. The primary advantage of a low-resolution color proof is cost; it is much less expensive to print a composite color image on a single page of high-quality paper than to run film negatives and compose them into a high-resolution color proof. Compare your costs: 50¢ per low-resolution page versus $100 per page for high-resolution Chromalin proofs.

Until you run your final negatives, changes at any stage are relatively quick and inexpensive to make. Consider the time and expense in the process of correcting a typographical error in conventional production methods: You would have to order the corrected type, wait for it to return from the typesetter, and incur delivery and production charges—and this does not include the time involved in replacing the defective type in the original layout. Using your computer, the change is made in short order and the correction can be reprinted on your desktop laser printer, creating a realistic, comprehensive proof that looks very much like the final product.

Digital files are consistent across all phases of production. The same file will be used to create your low-resolution proof and your high-resolution final production art—all without any program modification to the file from the many (likely) proofs to final film output.

Creating the Layout

In the conventional production world, in order to produce proofs and negatives, you must first lay out all the elements that will appear in your document. The type must be accurately positioned and composed; images must be placed and cropped with their itinerant production methods defined; and illustrations and artwork must be created, sized, and positioned. In order to make this camera-ready, all the individual components must be positioned on a stiff surface (usually special production paperboard) and solid color areas must be mechanically broken out and separated using thin films of amberlith or rubylith. An overlay is usually affixed to the whole assembly to indicate color breaks and to specify colors that are to be matched.

This entire assembly is then photographed in layers using a production camera to create a negative for each separate color and the base art. Images and photographs requiring special effects or treatments such as color separation or special halftone effects must be photographed separately and then mechanically composed into the final negatives (see Figure 1.9).

FIGURE 1.9 Composite image of a negative page.

Comps and Thumbnails

Before committing time, expense, and energy on a complete layout, you'll need to conceptualize your work by creating rough thumbnail sketches. Thumbnail sketches give a rough idea of what you visualize as the final product. It can help define a creative direction and technique that, in turn, gives your client a tool to help direct an effective creative approach and gives your service bureau an idea of the production requirements so that it can begin to estimate expenses.

At the very early stages of production, the initial comprehensive *roughs* (rough sketches) and thumbnails are still best created with pencils and markers for speed and agility. However, once you start creating a document on the computer, you can build on and edit this document into the final finished file without excessive duplication of effort (see Figures 1.10 and 1.11).

List the steps in the correct order...

- ☐ Create final layout on computer
- ☐ Choose creative direction in meeting with client
- ☐ Proof work
- ☐ Create final production artwork on computer
- ☐ Create thumbnail sketches and comps
- ☐ Proof work
- ☐ Get approval for work from client
- ☐ Proof printing
- ☐ Proof work
- ☐ Proof work
- ☐ Get final approval for work from client
- ☐ Send proofed project to service bureau or printer
- ☐ Proof work
- ☐ Print work
- ☐ Create new comprehensive layout with client changes
- ☐ Proof work
- ☐ Proof work
- ☐ Create comprehensive rough layout on computer

FIGURE 1.10 A quiz. Can you put the prepress steps in the right order?

Proof, proof, proof your work...

1. Choose creative direction in meeting with client
2. Create thumbnail sketches and comps
3. Proof work
4. Create comprehensive rough layout on computer
5. Proof work
6. Get approval for work from client
7. Create new comprehensive layout with client changes
8. Proof work
9. Create final layout on computer
10. Proof work
11. Get final approval for work from client
12. Proof work
13. Create final production artwork on computer
14. Proof work
15. Send proofed project to service bureau or printer
16. Print work
17. Proof printing

FIGURE 1.11 Quiz answers: The moral is proof, proof, proof.

Conventional vs. Digital Production Methods

While the major objective is still to get the ink onto the paper in the correct proportions and in the correct positions on a page, the techniques for realizing this objective have changed significantly in the past ten years. Every step in the process still involves a high level of precision, but the tools to create this level of precision have changed considerably, and they continue to change as the technology evolves.

Instead of a collection of very mechanical and chemical-intensive tools such as knives, wax, sprays, inks, and pens, the designer or production artist today has all of the functionality of these tools in a single piece of equipment: the computer. Your computer is thousands of times more precise than conventional handtools. Computers offer versatility and capability that was previously available only through expensive and time-consuming outside services.

Using computers, the designer or production artist can produce more work in less time and explore more design possibilities than was ever possible using conventional production methods. Changes are fast, easy, and much less expensive than before. The designer can try several different versions, colors, designs, effects, and typestyles in a project before committing to final output.

For example, consider some common and very simple editorial changes as shown in Figure 1.12.

FIGURE 1.12 Same common editorial corrections.

In the conventional graphic production world, the changes mentioned here would take a minimum of 24 hours to complete, would probably incur a rush charge here and there, and would still be susceptible to further changes. Let's take a look at what's involved in making the changes shown here. We'll also assume that all the steps necessary for these changes are initiated on the same day.

Resetting the type for the headline would probably be done overnight at your local typesetter. If you and your typesetter are smart, you'll order a few different variations on the reset of the headline (see Figure 1.13).

HeadLine
HeadLine
HeadLine
HeadLine
HeadLine
HeadLine

FIGURE 1.13 Headline variations.

The typesetter should be able to process the whole job under the same invoice, saving you a few dollars.

To adjust the contrast and background elements of the photo, you'll need to first send the original photo out to an airbrush studio or photographic studio for some lab work. In this case, since the changes indicated involve direct manipulation of the image itself, airbrush retouching may be necessary. It will involve considerable mechanical effort by a technician.

To reproduce the photograph at the new size, you'll need to get a few stats shot at different sizes (and the correct halftone value) (see Figure 1.14).

You may also want to have the logo shot at a few different sizes at the same time. If your typesetter has this capability in-house, you may be able to have this done at the same time and place as your typesetting, saving yourself a trip and a delivery charge.

FIGURE 1.14 Get a stat of the logo.

Now for the real time-consumer: You'll have to recompose all the newly revised elements onto the same page. Keep in mind that when there's more than one person involved in the approval process, there's bound to be a few extra revisions required. Count on laying your production out a few more times over the course of the next two or three meetings to make sure everyone's happy.

Using your computer, you can make all of these changes quickly and easily. Most of the changes requested can be accomplished in your page-layout program. For example, adjusting your headline type is as simple as choosing a few menu options and typing in some new values for kerning (see Figures 1.15 and 1.16).

FIGURE 1.15 First kerning selection.

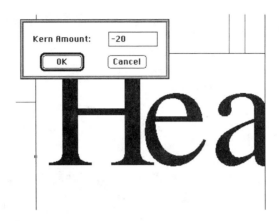

FIGURE 1.16 Second kerning selection.

The photograph is easily and quickly scanned using a desktop scanner (see Figure 1.17) and saved as a TIFF file.

FIGURE 1.17 A desktop scanner.

Changes to the photograph are easily accomplished using a software product called Photoshop (see Figure 1.18).

FIGURE 1.18 Changes to the image in Photoshop.

The retouched image is then imported into the page-layout document (see Figure 1.19). The page-layout software controls the halftone line screen frequency output of the image.

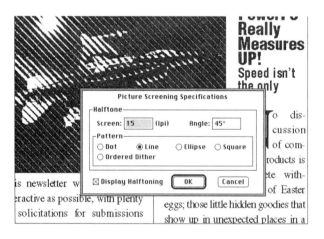

FIGURE 1.19 Sizing the image.

The image can be easily resized and repositioned within the page-layout software (see Figure 1.20).

FIGURE 1.20 Sizing with the measurements palette.

Naturally, the logo is resized and repositioned with the same simple menu commands and/or keystrokes (see Figure 1.21).

FIGURE 1.21 Correcting the page.

In fact, in just a few short minutes, you might even create a completely different page layout by rearranging all the elements on the page (see Figures 1.22

and 1.23). All it takes is a few simple clicks of the mouse and a few minutes of your time.

FIGURE 1.22 A page layout.

FIGURE 1.23 Another page layout.

FIGURE 1.24 Changes are instantaneous and cost next to nothing.
On top of it all, they are easily accomplished.

The Business of Prepress

Here's the one overriding issue surrounding the value of using a computer to produce camera-ready art for printing production: time. You've heard the saying, "Time is money." Time wasted is money lost. If you're spending time running around and duplicating efforts to get your work produced, you're losing the money you could be earning doing other projects. Computers help you perform your work much faster, more easily, and at a cost savings to you (and your client). Using the computer can help you get more work done faster and allow you more time to be more versatile and creative.

Time is also cumulative. If a computer can help you produce more work faster, then it makes sense that a faster computer will help you produce more work even faster than that. This is especially true ifyou find yourself working late on Friday evenings to finish your

23

unfinished projects. Imagine if you owned a computer that was only twenty percent faster than the computer you currently own. You could be finishing your work Thursday and taking Friday off. Or, if over-achievement is in your genes, you could be making a few more sales calls and chasing down more clients on Friday. Pay your mortgage off early, retire young, and live comfortably in a place where you used to only vacation. Time is cumulative. Every investment in any practices that save you time pays for itself and builds up "time-equity" that you can use for other objectives.

Summary

Prepress production is the art and science of preparing artwork for the printing process. This involves precise manipulation of type and images on a page to create negatives, from which plates will be made using a photo-mechanical process. The plates on a printing press then transfer ink from a reservoir to the paper passing through the press.

Using a computer to produce camera-ready art affords the designer or production artist incredible precision and versatility. Creating a final page layout for any publication is now a much easier and more efficient process than was ever possible before. From your regular thumbnail sketches, you can now move to a much more comprehensive layout for approval by your client before committing your work to final film negatives. Right from the outset, you are creating work that is ultimately thousands of times more precise than anything you could create by hand. The production process is more versatile, more easily corrected, and most importantly, more profitable.

Chapter 2

PostScript

- ❄ What is PostScript?
- ❄ How does it work?
- ❄ PostScript features and benefits
- ❄ Where, when, and how to use PostScript
- ❄ PostScript drawing programs
- ❄ PostScript and color
- ❄ PostScript versus non-PostScript typefaces
- ❄ Summary and tips
- ❄ Tip review

What is PostScript?

Chances are that when you first started using computers to produce graphics, the term *PostScript* was one of the more prominent words that came up when discussing capabilities. Do all computers have PostScript capabilities? Is PostScript in the computer or in the printer? Do I absolutely have to use PostScript in producing computer art?

Almost every computer-related product for use with computer-graphics production today will have the word PostScript listed somewhere among its features. PostScript compatibility has become a necessity for most high-resolution output uses. High-resolution laser printers need to have a version of PostScript *hard-wired*, (or built into) their CPU logic boards in order to interpret the PostScript data that are being composed and sent from the page-layout or drawing software on your computer.

PostScript is a page-description language developed by Adobe Systems, Inc. It provides a standardized description method for all items on a page, including text and graphics. It can be expressed as an object-oriented tool, allowing drawing programs to define all the attributes of objects that appear in an image. For example, shapes can have outlines, or *strokes*, defined in terms of halftone, color, and weight (see Figures 2.1 and 2.2). (Most PostScript drawing programs allow you to define strokes in increments of 0.001 of any unit of measure.) Shapes can also be filled with shades of gray, colors, graduated tints, and patterns, all of which can be further defined as spot or process color, overprints, or knockouts.

FIGURE 2.1 Each two-dimensional point in a PostScript document is defined as an x-y location in th3 image area.

Object attributes defined:

4 point black **stroke**,

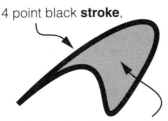

filled with 25% of black halftone

FIGURE 2.2 Elements of a shape in a PostScript document can
be defined with precise values for stroke weight and fill color.

PostScript describes to your printing device the location and attributes of
every image that will print on your page. This includes all artwork and
text. Letterforms for typefaces are shapes that have been created by an
artist using a drawing program; each shape is then assigned a specific key-
stroke. Like all PostScript objects, they are defined as points connected by
lines and *Bézier* curves and are then filled with defined colors and shades.

This may sound like a complex task, but what is really taking place in
this situation is simply one computer talking to another. There is actually a
sophisticated computer built into every PostScript-compatible printer, and
the computer "on board" inside the printer is exchanging information
with the desktop computer in a common binary computer language. The
printer's manufacturer has licensed the right to use a PostScript interpreter
developed by the Adobe Corporation on the logic board inside the printer,
allowing it to easily interpret and translate the PostScript instructions into
a high-resolution image on the page.

PostScript is a fairly comprehensive language with various dialects
and revisions constantly under development. In speaking with various
high-resolution output service bureaus, you will hear references to the
various versions of their RIP (raster image processor) devices that interpret
PostScript code into camera-ready images. Adobe released its newest version
of PostScript to the general masses in 1993. Named "PostScript Level 2,"
the new version enhanced the performance of PostScript-compatible output
devices, making high-resolution output more reliable.

How Does PostScript Work?

At its heart, PostScript uses the same principles found in basic two-dimensional plane geometry to determine the location of points in an illustration based on simple x- and y-coordinates. Connecting these points are straight lines and Bezier curves outlining shapes.

Raw PostScript code exists as textual instructions to the printer (see Figure 2.3). PostScript drawing programs then "interpret" the code into a graphical representation on your computer screen, so you can see the results of your work as you create it without having to be familiar with the actual programming language.

```
/Version 0 def
/Revision 0 def
/bdef {bind def} bind def
/ldef {load def} bdef
/xdef {exch def} bdef
/_K {3 index add neg dup 0 lt {pop 0} if 3 1 roll} bdef
/_k /setcmybcolor where
{/setcmybcolor get} {{1 sub 4 1 roll _K _K _K setrgbcolor pop} bind} ifelse def
/g {/_b xdef /p {_b setgray} def} bdef
/G {/_B xdef /P {_B setgray} def} bdef
/k {/_b xdef /_y xdef /_m xdef /_c xdef /p {_c _m _y _b _k} def} bdef
/K {/_B xdef /_Y xdef /_M xdef /_C xdef /P {_C _M _Y _B _k} def} bdef
```

FIGURE 2.3a An example of PostScript code.

Here is a simple shape created in Adobe Illustrator as it appears on the screen when it is created, with its corresponding screen image preview for import into other programs and the actual PostScript code that describes it to the printer.

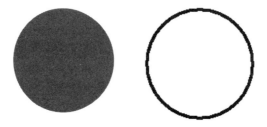

FIGURE 2.3b The shape described by the PostScript code below and its preview.

```
/Adobe_Illustrator_1.1 dup 100 dict def load begin
/Version 0 def
/Revision 0 def
/bdef {bind def} bind def
/ldef {load def} bdef
/xdef {exch def} bdef
/_K {3 index add neg dup 0 lt {pop 0} if 3 1 roll} bdef
/_k /setcmybcolor where
{/setcmybcolor get} {{1 sub 4 1 roll _K _K _K setrgbcolor
pop} bind} ifelse def
/g {/_b xdef /p {_b setgray} def} bdef
/G {/_B xdef /P {_B setgray} def} bdef
/k {/_b xdef /_y xdef /_m xdef /_c xdef /p {_c _m _y _b _k}
def} bdef
/K {/_B xdef /_Y xdef /_M xdef /_C xdef /P {_C _M _Y _B _k}
def} bdef
/d /setdash ldef
/_i currentflat def
/i {dup 0 eq {pop _i} if setflat} bdef
/j /setlinejoin ldef
/J /setlinecap ldef
/M /setmiterlimit ldef
/w /setlinewidth ldef
/_R {.25 sub round .25 add} bdef
/_r {transform _R exch _R exch itransform} bdef
/c {_r curveto} bdef
/C /c ldef
/v {currentpoint 6 2 roll _r curveto} bdef
/V /v ldef
/y {_r 2 copy curveto} bdef
/Y /y ldef
/l {_r lineto} bdef
/L /l ldef
/m {_r moveto} bdef
/_e [] def
/_E {_e length 0 ne {gsave 0 g 0 G 0 i 0 J 0 j 1 w 10 M [] 0 d
/Courier 20 0 0 1 z [0.966 0.259 -0.259 0.966
_e 0 get _e 2 get add 2 div _e 1 get _e 3 get add 2 div] e
_f t T grestore} if} bdef
/_fill {{fill} stopped
{/_e [pathbbox] def /_f (ERROR: can't fill, increase flatness)
def n _E} if} bdef
/_stroke {{stroke} stopped
{/_e [pathbbox] def /_f (ERROR: can't stroke, increase
flatness) def n _E} if} bdef
/n /newpath ldef
```

```
/N /n ldef
/F {p _fill} bdef
/f {closepath F} bdef
/S {P _stroke} bdef
/s {closepath S} bdef
/B {gsave F grestore S} bdef
/b {closepath B} bdef
/_s /ashow ldef
/_S {(?) exch {2 copy 0 exch put pop dup false charpath
currentpoint _g setmatrix
_stroke _G setmatrix moveto 3 copy pop rmoveto} forall pop
pop pop n} bdef
/_A {_a moveto _t exch 0 exch} bdef
/_L {0 _l neg translate _G currentmatrix pop} bdef
/_w {dup stringwidth exch 3 -1 roll length 1 sub _t mul add
exch} bdef
/_z [{0 0} bind {dup _w exch neg 2 div exch neg 2 div} bind
{dup _w exch neg exch neg} bind] def
/z {_z exch get /_a xdef /_t xdef /_l xdef exch findfont
exch scalefont setfont} bdef
/_g matrix def
/_G matrix def
/_D {_g currentmatrix pop gsave concat _G currentmatrix
pop} bdef
/e {_D p /t {_A _s _L} def} bdef
/r {_D P /t {_A _S _L} def} bdef
/a {_D /t {dup p _A _s P _A _S _L} def} bdef
/o {_D /t {pop _L} def} bdef
/T {grestore} bdef
/u {} bdef
/U {} bdef
/Z {findfont begin currentdict dup length dict begin
{1 index /FID ne {def} {pop pop} ifelse} forall /FontName
exch def dup length 0 ne
{/Encoding Encoding 256 array copy def 0 exch {dup type
/nametype eq
{Encoding 2 index 2 index put pop 1 add} {exch pop} ifelse}
forall} if pop
currentdict dup end end /FontName get exch definefont pop}
bdef
end
```

Here is a more complex shape, with corresponding PostScript code (see Figure 2.4). While the number of lines of code required to describe it to the printer is substantially increased, remember that computers (both on your desktop and inside the printer) interpret this information very quickly to render the image.

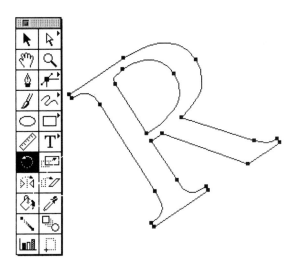

FIGURE 2.4 A more complex image with corresponding code.

```
/Version 0 def
/Revision 0 def
/bdef {bind def} bind def
/ldef {load def} bdef
/xdef {exch def} bdef
/_K {3 index add neg dup 0 lt {pop 0} if 3 1 roll} bdef
/_k /setcmybcolor where
{/setcmybcolor get} {{1 sub 4 1 roll _K _K _K setrgbcolor
pop} bind} ifelse def
/g {/_b xdef /p {_b setgray} def} bdef
/G {/_B xdef /P {_B setgray} def} bdef
/k {/_b xdef /_y xdef /_m xdef /_c xdef /p {_c _m _y _b _k}
def} bdef
/K {/_B xdef /_Y xdef /_M xdef /_C xdef /P {_C _M _Y _B _k}
def} bdef
/d /setdash ldef
/_i currentflat def
/i {dup 0 eq {pop _i} if setflat} bdef
/j /setlinejoin ldef
/J /setlinecap ldef
```

```
/M /setmiterlimit ldef
/w /setlinewidth ldef
/_R {.25 sub round .25 add} bdef
/_r {transform _R exch _R exch itransform} bdef
/c {_r curveto} bdef
/C /c ldef
/v {currentpoint 6 2 roll _r curveto} bdef
/V /v ldef
/y {_r 2 copy curveto} bdef
/Y /y ldef
/l {_r lineto} bdef
/L /l ldef
/m {_r moveto} bdef
/_e [] def
/_E {_e length 0 ne {gsave 0 g 0 G 0 i 0 J 0 j 1 w 10 M []
0 d
/Courier 20 0 0 1 z [0.966 0.259 -0.259 0.966
_e 0 get _e 2 get add 2 div _e 1 get _e 3 get add 2 div] e
_f t T grestore} if} bdef
/_fill {{fill} stopped
{/_e [pathbbox] def /_f (ERROR: can't fill, increase flat-
ness) def n _E} if} bdef
/_stroke {{stroke} stopped
{/_e [pathbbox] def /_f (ERROR: can't stroke, increase flat-
ness) def n _E} if} bdef
/n /newpath ldef
/N /n ldef
/F {p _fill} bdef
/f {closepath F} bdef
/S {P _stroke} bdef
/s {closepath S} bdef
/B {gsave F grestore S} bdef
/b {closepath B} bdef
/_s /ashow ldef
/_S {(?) exch {2 copy 0 exch put pop dup false charpath
currentpoint _g setmatrix
_stroke _G setmatrix moveto 3 copy pop rmoveto} forall pop
pop pop n} bdef
/_A {_a moveto _t exch 0 exch} bdef
/_L {0 _l neg translate _G currentmatrix pop} bdef
/_w {dup stringwidth exch 3 -1 roll length 1 sub _t mul add
exch} bdef
/_z [{0 0} bind {dup _w exch neg 2 div exch neg 2 div} bind
{dup _w exch neg exch neg} bind] def
/z {_z exch get /_a xdef /_t xdef /_l xdef exch findfont
exch scalefont setfont} bdef
```

```
/_g matrix def
/_G matrix def
/_D {_g currentmatrix pop gsave concat _G currentmatrix
pop} bdef
/e {_D p /t {_A _s _L} def} bdef
/r {_D P /t {_A _S _L} def} bdef
/a {_D /t {dup p _A _s P _A _S _L} def} bdef
/o {_D /t {pop _L} def} bdef
/T {grestore} bdef
/u {} bdef
/U {} bdef
/Z {findfont begin currentdict dup length dict begin
{1 index /FID ne {def} {pop pop} ifelse} forall /FontName
exch def dup length 0 ne
{/Encoding Encoding 256 array copy def 0 exch {dup type
/nametype eq
{Encoding 2 index 2 index put pop 1 add} {exch pop} ifelse}
forall} if pop
currentdict dup end end /FontName get exch definefont pop}
bdef
end
```

It starts with an identifying header that describes the type of document, dates of creation, fonts needed, version of the creation software, document and software parameters, and generally everything needed to identify itself and its requirements to the receiving printer.

Header information might look like this:

```
%!PS-Adobe-2.0 EPSF-1.2
%%Creator:Adobe Illustrator(TM) 5.5
%%For: (Edison Carter) (Network23)
%%Title: (Untitled art 2)
%%CreationDate: (08/17/94) (10:53 AM)
%%DocumentProcessColors: Black
%%DocumentProcSets: Adobe_Illustrator_1.1 0 0
%%DocumentSuppliedProcSets: Adobe_Illustrator_1.1 0 0
%%BoundingBox:226 305 366 445
%%ColorUsage: Black&White
%%TemplateBox:306 396 306 396
%%TileBox: 30 31 582 761
%%DocumentPreview: Header
%%EndComments
%%BeginProcSet:Adobe_Illustrator_1.1 0 0
```

This is followed by the actual imaging instructions written in the PostScript language. This information will include the location and attributes of every object and elemental component on the page in a language that the printer understands and can interpret. Whenever the print command is given, this same type of information travels to the printer and is interpreted into the image that appears on the page.

For example, the following is a simple circle with a solid black fill (see Figure 2.5). The PostScript code needed to render this image to a high-resolution imaging device is the same for a desktop laser printer as it is for a maximum-resolution camera-ready output device. The PostScript language code that generates this image follows.

FIGURE 2.5 A circle with a solid fill.

```
0 0 72 0 360 arc
fill
showpage
```

Adding attributes simply changes the instructions that are given to the printing device (see Figure 2.6). Notice how the **fill** command is now preceded by a **setgray** command to fill the shape with a shade of gray instead of black.

FIGURE 2.6 A circle with 50% gray set.

```
0 0 72 0 360 arc
.5 setgray
fill
showpage
```

All the images displayed on your Macintosh computer screen are rendered using a method called "QuickDraw" that translates your PostScript instructions into recognizable graphic images on-screen. QuickDraw displays all the colors and shapes that are visible on a screen quickly and is the image medium that all Macintosh programs use to display their images.

PostScript Features and Benefits

Because it relies primarily on textual instructions that express mathematical equations to describe theoretical two-dimensional locations for points and objects (and because computers are very good at interpreting these mathematical instructions), PostScript is a very efficient medium for describing the shapes of letterforms and illustration objects. PostScript has become an accepted file format standard that can be universally transferred between systems without modification.

The PostScript-compatible printer and the computer are, in essence, speaking the same language, and this makes the transfer and interpretation of the information very efficient. PostScript images are efficient in terms of the amount of program code required to render them. Rather than describing the location and attributes of every pixel contained in an illustration or image, PostScript allows for the definition of objects and their attributes. For example, in a regular raster-type image, each pixel in an area must be defined, while in a similar PostScript image, only the location and attributes (which consist of anchor points, the paths that connect them, and fill attributes) of the object itself must be specified.

PostScript images are objects that can be defined; that is, you can give them specific attributes for line weights and color composition. These objects can be revised and edited after they are created, making it easy to make changes to any image without having to re-create them (see Figure 2.7).

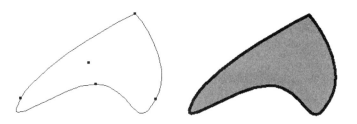

FIGURE 2.7 PostScript makes alternatives simple.

PostScript illustrations are *device-independent* for their resolution. This means that an EPS (Encapsulated PostScript) illustration printed on any lower-resolution (300-dot-per-inch or lower) printing device (such as Apple's LaserWriter) can also be printed on any higher-resolution device without any modifications to the file. The simple conversion to the high-resolution aspect of PostScript production makes it a perfect medium for creating very precise camera-ready artwork. Because it is digital, images and documents can easily be copied and stored without the usual chemistry and mechanical drawbacks of conventional production.

Instead of transporting and storing production art on illustration board with wax and rubylith overlays (see Figure 2.8), whole projects can be transported on a diskette that conveniently fits in your shirt pocket. No more X-acto knife injuries, inhaled spray-glue fumes, or tedious hours spent in darkrooms.

FIGURE 2.8 Different types of media.

Changes are faster and easier to make, and art production is thousands of times more precise than was ever possible before. Best of all, having a powerful computer system capable of all this on your desk is not the major financial challenge that it once was.

What does all this really mean to the designer or production artist? Imagine having all the benefits of a stat camera right on your desktop. Imagine sharing art without having to shoot photo-mechanical duplicates of all your camera-ready line art. Wouldn't it be great to make multiple copies and generations of your productions quickly and easily without any loss of quality whatsoever? These are some of the benefits of PostScript.

PostScript represents a fundamental shift in the distribution of resources needed to produce camera-ready artwork as compared with conventional prepress production.

Anyone with a desktop or portable computer using PostScript-compatible software can create high-quality, high-resolution, camera-ready artwork without having to make a significant investment in specialized imaging hardware such as typesetters and stat cameras. Because of this, there has been a change in the distribution of specialized technical skills and knowledge needed to create camera-ready or print-ready artwork, a difference that the industry is only now beginning to be able to balance.

In the past, a designer or production artist had several sources for the individual tasks required for print production. There were typesetters, camera operators, strippers, compositors, separators, and a host of other outside service providers. A smaller amount of knowledge about each of these specialized fields was required in order to interact with these service providers. Primarily, communications issues alone were required to define the results needed, not the actual mechanical issues to achieve those results. Now, with the capabilities presented by common desktop hardware and software solutions, the list of outside services required, while not eliminated completely, is significantly shortened. Of all the services mentioned here, most are now accomplished on the desktop, with the final product obtainable from a single outside source: the imaging service bureau.

With all these new capabilities comes a new higher level of responsibilities. The person creating the actual camera-ready artwork is now responsible for the quality and usefulness of that artwork. Herein lies the knowledge/time paradox, in which increased time to learn the nuts-and-bolts mechanics of production is required in order to take advantage of the time-saving benefits of desktop electronic graphics production. More knowledge and specialized technical skills are required of the desktop-graphics production artist than was necessary before these capabilities became available with computers. Powerful illustrations of this point are made in following chapters, where legal matters and prepress horror stories are presented.

When, Where, and How to Use PostScript?

If you're using a computer for graphic production, you're probably already using PostScript. Most laser printers have PostScript interpreters built into their logic boards. Your service bureau or printing-services provider, or whoever is taking care of your camera-ready output, is using PostScript to image your files on its imagesetter.

One of the remarkable aspects of the computer-graphics world is that you, the user, do not have to interface with, or even be aware of, how the program you're using interacts with the PostScript language. Everything you are working with on your screen is being translated for you to PostScript code in the background without your direct intervention. The raw PostScript code is then sent to your printer for interpretation and printing. A little knowledge about the process itself can help you troubleshoot and avoid potential production problems.

Do I Really Need PostScript?

PostScript is not an absolute requirement. In an effort to provide lower-cost and higher-resolution printers to new users, PostScript compatibility has been left out of some of the lower-end printers that are for sale today. While these printers still offer relatively high-resolution printing (360 dots per inch, or dpi), the capabilities and benefits of PostScript have been left out. These printers do not use PostScript to create their images at all; they rely entirely on Apple's proprietary QuickDraw rendering scheme to accomplish screen rendering and printing tasks (see Figures 2.9, 2.10, and 2.11). QuickDraw still allows for precise reproduction of typefaces using their own proprietary font-rendering technology called TrueType, which is discussed later in this chapter.

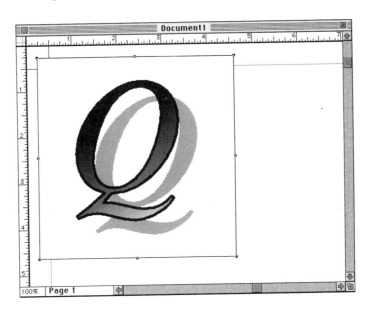

FIGURE 2.9 This is how the image will appear on your computer's monitor.

FIGURE 2.10 This is how the image will print on a non-PostScript printer.

FIGURE 2.11 This is how the image will print on a high-resolution output device, with more than 2100 dots per inch.

PostScript art printed using a non-PostScript printer will not have the fine resolution of which PostScript printers are capable. Non-PostScript printers may have fine resolution capabilities but lack the necessary engineering to interpret the instructions that encapsulated PostScript files include. There are some ways to get around this, which will allow you to make up somewhat for the lack of PostScript on your printer, but they require the use of several different software products (see Figure 2.12).

FIGURE 2.12 A screen image of a non-PostScript document.

This clean and precise EPS image will print at the computer's screen resolution when printed on a non-PostScript compatible printer (see Figure 2.13).

FIGURE 2.13 This is how Figure 2.12 will look printed on a non-PostScript printer.

Here's a slightly inconvenient and only moderately tedious way to improve the look of your EPS images on a non-PostScript printer such as Apple's StyleWriter inkjet printers:

1. After creating and saving your PostScript object-based image in the EPS format, launch your Adobe Photoshop image editing software and open your EPS file (see Figure 2.14).

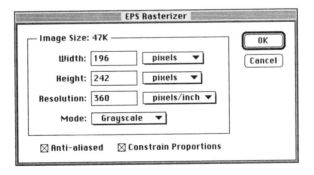

FIGURE 2.14 Opening an EPS file in Photoshop.

2. Set the pixel resolution of the new image to **360 dpi** (the maximum that your StyleWriter or other non-PostScript inkjet printer will print) and set the mode to **Grayscale**.

3. Convert the image to PICT format by choosing **Save as...** under the File menu, then choosing **PICT** as your format (see Figure 2.15).

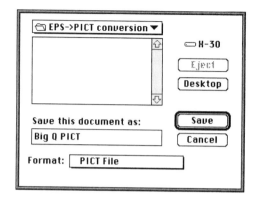

FIGURE 2.15 Save as PICT.

4. Quit Adobe Photoshop and launch your favorite page-layout program. Then import the new PICT image into your document (see Figure 2.16).

FIGURE 2.16 The final PICT image.

Your non-PostScript inkjet printer prints the grayscale image at its maximum resolution as cleanly and efficiently as it can. Note that the file size of your high-resolution PICT image may be much larger than your original EPS document.

PostScript File Formats

There are a few instances where knowing a little about the intricacies of PostScript will help you take best advantage of the system. One of those instances is in the area of file formats.

In order for a PostScript image to be imported to a page-layout program, it must first be saved (or converted) to an encapsulated PostScript image

(EPS). Encapsulating a PostScript image records more information to the header of the document and includes a screen-image preview of the document. Page-layout programs such as QuarkXPress and PageMaker will use this preview as a guide for placing the image and running text around it. While the program will display a PICT preview of the PostScript image, the program maintains a link with the original high-resolution PostScript image data, allowing it to reference that data to create the camera-ready image in the imagesetting device.

The important thing to remember about importing EPS images to your page-layout program is that the actual file for the imported image must be able to be found by the page-layout software while it is printing (see Figures 2.18 and 2.19). This means that when you send a file to your imaging service bureau, you must be sure to include it in the same folder as the page-layout document you are printing. If the maze file cannot be found, it will print as a low-resolution preview image as it appears on your computer screen. Most page-layout programs have the capability to warn the user if a file is missing or has been modified. Be sure to take advantage of this capability—your service bureau should also pay attention to this. Encourage its representative to call you as soon as possible if required files or fonts are missing.

FIGURE 2.17 Correctly rendered page where the high-resolution scan is available to the page-layout software, and incorrectly rendered snapshot of page without referenced PostScript illustrations.

43

FIGURE 2.18 Incorrectly rendered page; the page-layout software was unable to find the high-resolution information, so it rendered the image at the display resolution.

Most service bureaus will spend a good portion of their day on the telephone calling their clients to retrieve missing fonts or images. Save yourself (and your service bureau) time and money by checking your files before you send for output. Use the **Collect for output...** feature under the QuarkXPress File menu.

T I P

There are two basic subtypes of encapsulated PostScript files: object-based and pixel-based images. Object-based drawings that are created with PostScript drawing programs are particularly suited to technical renderings and line art. These images are primarily collections of defined objects on a page that, in most cases, can be quickly and efficiently printed because the objects are defined with textual mathematical data describing their x - and y - locations as well as any assigned elemental attributes on the page. Line art and technical renderings are especially efficient in this format because the objects created are precisely defined and take advantage of the imaging device's high-resolution capabilities.

Pixel-based PostScript images are grayscale images that have been converted to grayscale PostScript images. While they are indeed PostScript and can be imported into a PostScript drawing program, they are limited to the resolution at which they were scanned or saved. These images also require more processing work for the computer and imaging device, because the attributes and location of *each* pixel displayed must be defined and printed (see Figures 2.19

and 2.20). Pixel-based grayscale EPS conversions tend to occupy significantly more storage space than object-based EPS images, making them less convenient to store and transport. Once imported to a page-layout program, the halftone screen output of such images cannot be changed within the page-layout program, unlike regular grayscale TIFF images, which can be easily converted and changed outside of the program that created them.

FIGURE 2.19 The original pixel-based PostScript image as it will print.

FIGURE 2.20 Correctly rendered image, where the high-resolution scan is available to the page layout software, and incorrectly rendered snapshot of page without referenced scanned images. (next)

PostScript Drawing Programs

PostScript drawing programs offer powerful creation and manipulation tools for illustration. They can automate and streamline the effort of graphic design and production. They work by creating a graphical representation of the PostScript commands generated with the program. The interfaces are relatively intuitive with a fairly common palette of PostScript tools for precise editing of the objects you create.

One of the main strengths of PostScript drawing programs is the capability to create precise, smooth, and controllable Beziér curves connected by "anchor" points and definable paths (see Figure 2.21).

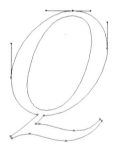

FIGURE 2.21 Object-based PostScript illustration as it is being created. Control and anchor points are connected by Beziér curve paths controlled by handles.

Curves can be easily altered without sacrificing pixel resolution. This technology enables the creation of clean and precise font outlines that lend themselves easily to creative graphic design (see Figures 2.22 through 2.24). Objects can then be defined as having specific halftone fills, lineweights and even precise blends.

FIGURE 2.22 The Beziér curves can be significantly altered.

FIGURE 2.23 Without altering the resolution.

FIGURE 2.24 And pulling the anchor points back
can bring the figure back to its original form.

PostScript objects can be scaled, rotated, and manipulated without affecting the resolution of the final output. That means that all the inherent problems with pixel-based graphic images are overcome with PostScript. You can rotate, scale, skew, and stretch an EPS image without affecting the resolution. Note how similar pixel-based and EPS images compare with each of the attendant changes mentioned (see Figures 2.25 and 2.26).

FIGURE 2.25 PostScript file as it would appear printed
on a high-resolution PostScript compatible printer.

FIGURE 2.26 PostScript file as it would appear printed on a non-PostScript printer.

There are plenty of choices in the drawing program market today. While "feature wars" escalate the number of bells and whistles on competing products, some new features have been known to cause problems with imagesetter RIPs. The best advice to follow to ensure problem-free output is to contact the imaging service bureau with which you regularly do business to find out which products reproduce with the least trouble.

PostScript and Color

PostScript objects can be defined for spot and process color. Most page-composition programs, like QuarkXPress, will recognize and accommodate color-defined PostScript objects, creating accurate separations of the individual negative plates with registration and crop marks to facilitate prepress production. Remember that when importing PostScript color images containing a specific color into your page-layout program, the same color—with the same name—must exist in the color palette of your page-layout document. This means that if you specify a particular Pantone color as part of your PostScript drawing, you must remember to include that same specific Pantone color in your page-layout document's color palette in order for the program to correctly print and separate your high-resolution negatives (see Figures 2.27 and 2.28).

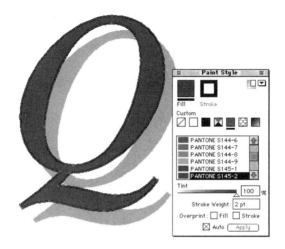

Figure 2.27 Pantone color selected for PostScript object.

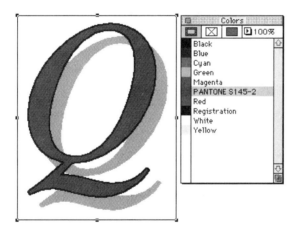

Figure 2.28 The Pantone color as it now automatically appears after being imported to the page-layout program. Remember to check all colors after import to assure proper color separation in production.

While the current versions of the two biggest page-layout products accommodate the import of EPS colors by automatically polling the EPS document on import and then adding the correct colors to the color palette, it is always a good idea to double-check the color palette and color list to make sure all colors and color names have been properly installed.

Remember, PostScript images imported into page-layout programs already have all their elements strictly defined by the program that created them. These definitions are not changeable after they are imported to your page-layout program. This is especially important if you are considering making changes to the default-trapping values in your page-layout software. Changing the trapping values of the individual color elements in your EPS graphic requires opening that image file in the program that created it and making changes there.

There are hardware and software tools available that automate the trapping process. Be sure to ask your imagesetting service bureau if they offer that service and which hardware/software is most effective for the type of format you're planning to image.

The Difference Between PostScript and Non-PostScript Typefaces

In the early days of Macintosh, there was only a small collection of screen fonts available for the system. In order for each size of a face to appear correctly on-screen there had to be a corresponding size for that face in the System folder. To display 12-point Helvetica, you had to have the 12-point Helvetica typeface installed in your system. If you wanted to display and print 24-point Helvetica, you had to install the 24-point size of Helvetica to your system.

When the early LaserWriters and other PostScript-compatible devices arrived on the scene, a new font-rendering technology had to be developed. The printers offered the capability to print large faces cleanly and precisely, but the font that displayed on the Macintosh screen would appear unwieldy and chunky, rendering the larger faces with blocky, jagged edges, "stair-stepping" the font's appearance on-screen. A collection of fonts was built into the printer's ROM chips to afford clean rendering of those typefaces (see Figures 2.29 through 2.31).

FIGURES 2.29 and 2.30 Without the appropriate font-rendering utility, this uppercase P renders as a blocky, stair-stepped image on screen, but still prints cleanly.

FIGURE 2.31 With the appropriate font-rendering utility, the same character appears cleanly, simplifying editing and control.

Eventually, Adobe introduced Adobe Type Manager (ATM) to allow for clean rendering of larger-scaled fonts on the screen no matter what size was specified. This also relieved the necessity of keeping a different font file for each size you wanted to render on-screen. ATM allowed for the use of a single screen font that rendered itself cleanly at any size using hints provided in a separate encrypted font file called a *printer font*, in the System folder.

The same technology is in use today with Adobe Type 1 scalable fonts, because ATM is still the preferred standard among professional users. The difference is only in the way the system software stores and controls fonts (see Figure 2.32). With Apple's System 7 and beyond, both screen and printer fonts are stored in a Fonts folder inside the System folder.

Fonts   Chicago   Chicago   Helvetica 12   Helve

FIGURE 2.32 A font suitcase from the Fonts folder in the System folder, a TrueType font file icon, a regular screen font icon and its accompanying Adobe PostScript Type 1 printer font referenced for accurate font rendering.

Eventually, Apple and Microsoft got together to develop a competing font-rendering scheme that simplified the rendering effort for the user but had definite drawbacks for the imaging service bureau. It was called TrueType.

Both TrueType and Type 1 fonts are capable of accurately rendering letterforms on-screen, and both are recognized by most PostScript drawing programs. However, there are some fundamental differences in the way that each is rendered, which may affect your choice of which to use in professional design and production.

The mathematics used to render curves and lines in TrueType use *quadratic* curves, while Adobe PostScript Type 1 fonts use simpler Bezier curves to render their letterforms. Simply put, Type 1 fonts are easier for your imagesetter to render because they use fewer control points, and the math used to calculate the curves is simpler for the printer to digest.

Current Apple LaserWriters have the necessary software to quickly render their TrueType fonts hard-wired into the ROMs on their logic boards. This makes it easier and faster for these printers to image TrueType fonts, and since Type 1 PostScript fonts are so much more efficient, there is no (supposedly) appreciable difference in printing times.

So why choose one over the other? There are several factors to consider when deciding which font technology to use in your production. Both technologies coexist fairly amicably. Following are some arguments for each.

The Case for TrueType

TrueType was developed as a competing font-rendering technology designed to afford people using non-PostScript-compatible printers the ability to display and print clean typefaces without using a PostScript interpreter or the PostScript page-description language.

TrueType uses a completely different rendering technique from PostScript to display and print fonts on your computer. It simplifies the installation and control of fonts by creating a single font suitcase containing all the information to render and display a given font. Naturally, this suitcase is larger than the average screen typeface, but since no printer font is required and no additional rendering software—like ATM—is required, it all balances out pretty equitably. The main difference that you should be concerned about is TrueType's rendering technique. TrueType requires roughly 25% more computing horsepower to render and print at high resolutions. In addition, the rendering scheme (which uses quadratic curves instead of Bezier curves) prints each shape as a high-resolution bit-map image. Sometimes this will cause an imagesetter to "hang" or "crash," thus forcing money-losing nonproductive time to be expended on your job.

One way Apple is compensating for this drawback is by hard-wiring the capability to render and print TrueType fonts into their LaserWriter printers, thereby keeping TrueType and Adobe Type 1 fonts on a relatively even footing. This ensures that genuine Apple LaserWriters will always be able to manage and print TrueType fonts easily and efficiently, but that changes significantly when one is outputting from almost any other high-resolution device.

Improvements in memory management and processing speed are sure to alleviate the problem as systems grow and mature, however, and as long as PostScript exists in the RIP of your imagesetter, there will always be an advantage to using genuine PostScript typefaces and rendering technology for high-resolution output. Don't be shy about asking your service bureau which technology works best.

TrueType was originally billed by Apple as "Font Democracy," affording everyone the capability to print and display clean fonts and typefaces regardless of whether they could afford an expensive PostScript-compatible printer. However, for graphics professionals and output service bureaus, it looks a lot more like "Font Socialism," forcing everyone into the lowest common denominator of slow rendering and printing times and larger file sizes.

The true test of TrueType is to ask your service bureau which fonts create the least problems for them and which they would prefer that you include with your work. In addition, ask how much more a job will cost if the document hangs the imagesetter for any length of time and how much time is spent and money lost restarting a crashed imagesetter due to competing font technologies.

The Case for PostScript

PostScript Type 1 typefaces have several advantages to offer the professional designer or production artist. Perhaps the most compelling is that PostScript was first on the scene and was quickly adopted by the industry. Service bureaus have already standardized on Type 1 fonts and Adobe Type Manager. Adobe continues to actively support professional font design and production in-house, selling very high-quality and reliable fonts. They come at a premium cost, but are preferred by almost everyone in the industry.

Adobe Type 1 fonts print more efficiently on high-resolution imagesetters that use the industry-standard Adobe PostScript RIP, speeding up processing time for the service bureau operator. Both products are created and rendered using the same language, making for fewer imaging problems.

Most PostScript drawing programs can now efficiently translate both Type 1 and TrueType fonts into outlines. Conversion of either font-rendering scheme is quick and easy in any drawing program; however, TrueType letterforms often contain extraneous control points that do nothing but increase image complexity and resultant processing time. Watch for this inadequacy and be ready for the inherent problems it represents.

Caveat Emptor

Competing font technologies that coexist in your system, especially files with the same name, will invariably create headaches for you when you least expect it. Any service bureau will tell you that having both PostScript and TrueType technologies present in your system is an open invitation to disaster. It's a good idea to decide which is best for you and to standardize on it (see Figure 2.33). That doesn't mean that you can never use TrueType in your system; just be prudent and aware, and don't take too many unnecessary chances.

FIGURE 2.33 Note that the ATM-rendered font on the left uses fewer defining control points than the less efficiently rendered TrueType font on the left. The TrueType font requires more processing effort for the printer to render at higher resolutions.

There are plenty of vendors out there ready to sell you a CD-ROM filled with thousands of typefaces for only $49.95. Beware of these collections if you feel tempted by the price, for all the reasons listed here.

As always, with any issues that affect prepress production, consult with your service bureau to determine its recommendation for which kind of typefaces you should use. It will have the experience necessary to make an objective recommendation.

Summary

PostScript is an advanced page-description language that allows for device-independent high-resolution production across most desktop computer platforms and software products. It works by describing to a PostScript-compatible printer the locations and attributes of two-dimensional graphic objects on a page. This affords high-resolution results across several printing devices without modifications to the file itself.

PostScript, with its concomitant document creation and manipulation software, affords the digital graphics production artist an efficient medium that is easy to manipulate and output. This means that the graphics production artist may create a PostScript file using a variety of drawing and page-layout software products and print the file at camera-ready resolutions on a variety of printing devices without having to modify the document file in any way.

PostScript has become an almost universally accepted file format for high-resolution graphics production, and it works almost transparently in almost any graphics application. Because the actual PostScript commands are automatically translated and interpreted by the various programs without user intervention, PostScript is easy to use and has become prevalent as a file-format standard in the industry.

Most PostScript files are saved in the EPS (encapsulated PostScript) file format, which allows for a PICT preview of the PostScript document for importing into other programs that accept the EPS format. This format saves information about all the elemental objects in the EPS document, including two-dimensional location on the page and attributes such as halftone screen values and densities, process and spot color separation, and line weights.

Systems using PostScript Type 1 typefaces and Adobe Type Manager software may accurately render typefaces for precise layout and design. The major competition for Type 1 typefaces is Apple's and Microsoft's proprietary TrueType font format, which allows for high-resolution rendering and printing of typefaces to printers and systems that do not include PostScript. While there is great debate about the two competing font-rendering methods, it is a good idea to consult with your imaging service bureau as to which font technology will provide the best results based on your type usage and desired output devices.

Tip Review

* As always, with any issues that affect prepress production, consult the people at your service bureau to determine their recommendation for the typefaces you should use. They have the experience to make an objective recommendation.

* The true test of TrueType is to ask the people at your service bureau which fonts create the fewest problems for them and which they would prefer that you include with your work. Ask how much extra a job will cost if the document hangs the imagesetter for any length of time and approximately how much time is spent and money lost restarting a crashed imagesetter due to competing font technologies.

✳ There are hardware and software tools available that automate the trapping process. Be sure to ask your imagesetting service bureau if it offers such a service and which would be most effective for the type of format you're planning to image.

✳ Most service bureaus will spend a good portion of their day on the telephone calling their clients to retrieve missing fonts or images. Save yourself (and your service bureau) time and money by checking your files before sending them for output. Use the **Collect for output...** feature under the QuarkXPress File menu.

✳ There are plenty of choices in the drawing program market today. While "feature wars" escalate the number of bells and whistles on competing products, some new features have been known to cause problems with imagesetter RIPs. Your best advice to ensure problem-free output is to contact the imaging service bureau with which you regularly do business and find out which products reproduce with the fewest problems.

✳ While the current versions of the two biggest page-layout products accommodate the import of EPS colors by automatically polling the EPS document on import and then adding the correct colors to the color palette, it is always a good idea to double-check the color palette and color list to make sure all colors and correct color names have been properly installed.

✳ When saving your PostScript drawings for placement into a page-layout program, save in the EPS file format.

✳ You can import QuarkXPress documents into other page-layout programs one page at a time by choosing the **Save page as EPS...** option under the File menu. This will save the entire page as a PostScript picture document. There is one caveat, however: the EPS file that results will still need to reference any embedded images and typefaces that it contains.

Chapter 3

The Concepts

* Process color explained
* Mechanical prepress color separation
* Conventional versus digital capabilities
* When to do it yourself (and when leave it to your service bureau)
* Summary

Process Color Explained

The concepts behind creating accurate color on paper are fairly straightforward. The printing industry has been using a method called *process color separation* to simulate a full range of colors to reproduce photography and match colors on the printed page since the beginning of offset lithography. Technological advances have brought about changes in the materials and practices over the years, but the basic procedure remains largely unchanged today.

Briefly, the process by which full color is created for printing involves separation of all color images in a publication into four basic "process" colors: cyan, magenta, yellow, and black.

Process colors and process color separations are often referred to as *CMYK process*. Note that the four letters are the initial letters of the four process colors: *c*-yan, *m*-agenta, *y*-ellow, and blac*k*. The letter *K* is used to indicate black for two reasons: *K* is unique to black among the four color names, and you are less likely to get confused and think of it as blue.

Mechanical Prepress Color Separation

A plate is made for each process color. Each separate ink color is then applied to the page in series, starting with yellow, then magenta, then blue (cyan), and finally black. Some sophisticated projects require the application of a fifth or sixth color, or a special varnish in addition to the four process colors, to create special printing effects (see Figures 3.1a through d).

FIGURE 3.1 The 4-color picture.

FIGURE 3.1a The yellow plate.

FIGURE 3.1b The magenta plate.

FIGURE 3.1c The cyan plate.

FIGURE 3.1d The black plate.

The process colors are over-printed onto each other in varying halftone densities and at different angles, to simulate a full range of colors such as would be found in reproducing a color photograph using the four basic process colors. This creates the illusion of a full range of colors and can allow for the creation of colors that can be precisely controlled and matched (see Figures 3.2 and 3.3).

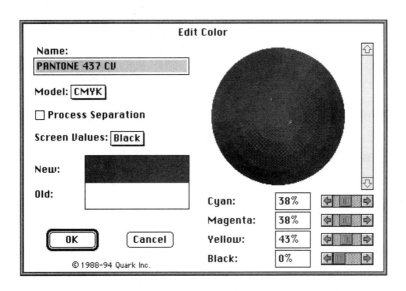

FIGURE 3.2 This color was matched using a mixture of the four process colors in the following densities: 38%, 38%, 43%, 0%.

Until recently, producing these effects involved a very labor-intensive process that required significant investment in equipment and technical expertise. Because of the expense involved, these services would most likely be performed by out-of-house service providers such as specialty service bureaus and high-end printing companies. Control over the final product, the time required for production, deliveries, responsibilities, and expense all went out the door to the various service providers with the project.

Conventional Versus Digital Capabilities

Current technology allows most (if not all) of these capabilities to remain on the designer's or the production artist's desk throughout the process. Typography, production photography, image manipulation, even color separation are now available as in-house capabilities, using relatively inexpensive hardware that is available through your local computer reseller. All the control (and responsibility) remains at the designer's desk instead of requiring the use of outside services.

As if that weren't enough, there are also new capabilities that allow for a depth of creativity and versatility that was not possible until recently. The designer and production artist can now retouch images, apply custom halftone effects, and even create new forms of art. Last-minute changes and revisions are not only convenient, they are easy to accomplish and easier than ever to afford.

Recording images for halftone reproduction was accomplished through the use of large floor-standing stat cameras (see Figure 3.3). The camera recorded the flat image onto photosensitive paper, which was then chemically processed to create either film or paper output. Special halftone effects were performed by a very skilled technician using special materials.

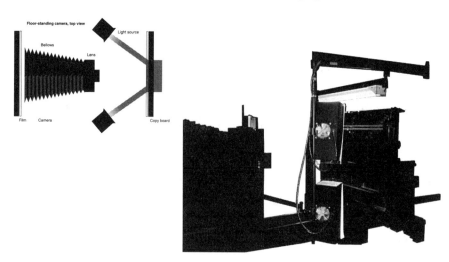

FIGURE 3.3 A floor-standing camera.

Today, the designer can record high-resolution images using a desktop flatbed scanner (see Figure 3.4) that costs a fraction of the cost of a stat camera. The image is digitally recorded onto magnetic media without the trouble and expense of chemical processing. Because the image is digital, manipulating the image is easy and efficient using software products such as Adobe Photoshop (see Figure 3.5).

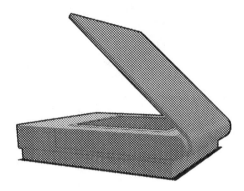

FIGURE 3.4 A desktop scanner.

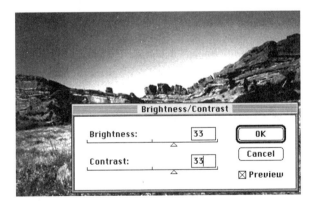

FIGURE 3.5 Changing grey-scale values in Photoshop.

The final results are comparable, and because the capability exists entirely on the desk of the designer, a more versatile and controllable product is available.

Similarly, with color images, it was not very long ago that the only source for full-color separation was a large and expensive drum-type scanner (see Figure 3.6). It required a skilled technician to operate and a great deal of money to purchase and maintain.

FIGURE 3.6 A high-resolution drum scanner with operator.

Today, of course, most of the functionality of higher-end scanners can be obtained in a desktop flatbed unit at a fraction of the cost. Once an image is saved in its digital format, the designer or production artist has almost unlimited control in manipulation and composition of the final image.

Image scanning, retouching, and manipulation services costing hundreds (or even thousands) of dollars are now available to the designer or production artist using the same versatile piece of hardware that is laying out the final page composition (and creating precise PostScript drawings, new typefaces, and page designs). It's an exciting time to be involved in this industry.

When to Do it Yourself (and When to Leave it to Your Service Bureau)

With any new empowering technology, there is always the dark possibility that it will fall into the wrong hands and be controlled by madmen and lunatics. Such is the case with desktop color capabilities. It's entirely possible for a less-than-qualified operator with insufficient experience or education to create less-than-ideal results. Remember, with all these new capabilities, there is also the responsibility of knowing how to use the tools.

The responsibility of creating great output is on the desk of the production artist. However, the ability to create great work is now more dependent on knowledge than on hardware. Learning more about the software tools can go a long way toward getting the best possible output and can compensate for hardware shortcomings (see Figures 3.7 and 3.8a-c).

FIGURE 3.7 A simple scan in Photoshop.

Filter	Select	Window
Sharpen	⌘F	iff (CMYK, 1:1)

Blur ▶
Distort ▶
Noise ▶
Pixelate ▶
Render ▶
Sharpen ▶ | Sharpen
Stylize ▶ | Sharpen Edges
Video ▶ | Sharpen More
Other ▶ | Unsharp Mask...

FIGURE 3.8a Photoshop Sharpen menu.

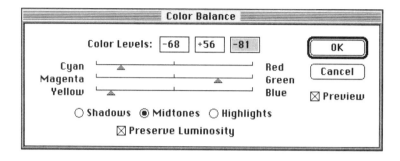

FIGURE 3.8b Photoshop color balance menu.

FIGURE 3.8c Corrected figure.

Color Production Techniques

Being able to scan and save a color image does not necessarily mean you will be able to reproduce a process color separation. Using your computer to create accurate color separations can be a simple task. Follow these easy steps:

1. After scanning your color image with your desktop scanner, open the image with Adobe Photoshop (see Figure 3.9).

FIGURE 3.9 Original scan.

2. Change the image format by choosing CMYK under the Mode menu. This will convert the computer's RGB (red-green-blue) display of the image to the CMYK standard, giving you a more accurate picture of how the image will print using the four-color process technique (see Figure 3.10).

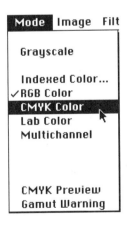

FIGURE 3.10 Change from RGB to CMYK in the Mode menu of Photoshop.

3. Make whatever color and image corrections are necessary to achieve the results you're after (see Figure 3.11). Remember that your screen display will vary slightly from the final printed image.

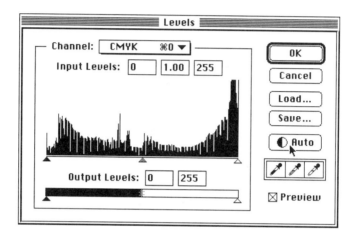

FIGURE 3.11 Make all necessary image corrections.

4. Choose **Save As...** (see Figure 3.12) under the File menu to change the file to a CMYK TIFF image (see Figure 3.13).

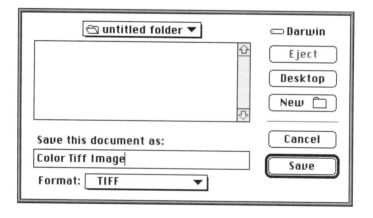

FIGURE 3.12 Save the file as a CMYK TIFF.

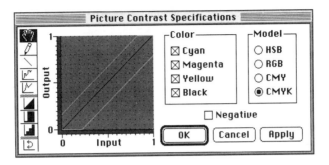

FIGURE 3.13 Changing CMYK contrasts.

5. Now your image has all the necessary data saved in a format that will separate onto each plate digitally. You can import it directly into your page-layout software for printing your color proofs.

TIP

While most page-layout programs offer the capability to adjust the color balance of any imported color TIFF image, it's usually a better idea to make all your color adjustments in your image-manipulation program. This ensures that less is lost in the translation between programs and translation to desktop color separation (DCS) files.

TIP

Be sure to remind your service bureau to convert the files to DCS format when they receive your disks. Converting your images to DCS format will occupy up to five times the file space as your basic CMYK TIFF images. Asking your service bureau to create the DCS files for you will keep your file space requirements lower for transportation to your service bureau.

Controlling Color

How can you be sure that the color that prints on the page will match the color you see on your computer screen? Or that the color that prints on your color-proofing system will match what finally ends up on the paper at the press? And how does that compare with what's displayed on your screen?

There are color-matching utilities on the market today to help you with this challenge. The concept is that each device that prints or displays colors does so to the best of its ability compared to an absolute color spectrum that is visible to the human eye (see Figures 3.14 and 3.15). For example, printed process colors created by mixing different densities of four process color inks are less likely to match colors in the purple end of the spectrum, and brilliant reds are somewhat muted due to the four-color printing process.

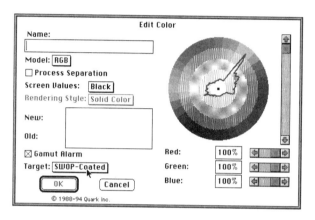

FIGURE 3.14 Assume that this color wheel is the complete spectrum of visible light. A sheet-fed web offset press is capable of accurately reproducing only the colors that appear inside the outline. But how do you know what colors will reproduce accurately?

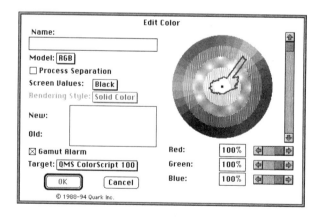

FIGURE 3.15 This example illustrates the color reproduction capabilities of the Apple Color StyleWriter Pro. Colors inside the outline will reproduce accurately.

If there were a software product that compensated for this inequity, displaying on your screen only what a target device is capable of printing, you might be able to make better decisions and choices in colors for your publications. Luckily for you, there is a solution available. With every color-capable device, Apple sends a system extension called *ColorSync* that is designed to aid in displaying accurate colors on-screen according to what each color-capable device will print.

ColorSync works by referring to a folder full of documents called *profiles* that the extension uses as a database of information about color-capable devices. For example, a profile for the Apple Color StyleWriter Pro would contain information about its ability to reproduce colors. Any application that is ColorSync-aware will be able to adjust the screen display of colors according to the target device's (in this case the Color StyleWriter Pro's) capabilities.

If you use different printing devices, getting your computer to accurately display colors according to that device's capabilities is as simple as dragging a small text file **Profile** into the Profiles folder in your System folder. Profiles are available from the manufacturers of each color printing device. Some come at a nominal fee, some are included free with the purchase of the device. Contact your device's manufacturer for information about availability and costs.

Controlling color and color balance in your images is a much simpler task if you have some idea of the outcome of your adjustments before you print the final negatives. A great example of this is found when you're using a program like Adobe Photoshop to adjust the color balance of a scanned image. The scanned image is saved in the RGB format; this perfect for displaying on computer screens and projection devices, but significantly different from CMYK, which is the printing standard for production art. The simplest way to illustrate this concept is to open any RGB-format image and change the mode to CMYK. You will see how the color character changes with the new mode.

Remember to change the color model and the target device for your output *before* you begin adjusting the color balance in your image. In any image-editing software, you can see how the entire character of your color image changes when you change the mode from RGB to CMYK. Avoid surprises in your output by choosing CMYK before you begin adjusting colors.

Traps, Chokes, and Spreads

Trapping is the practice of creating a small area of overlapping ink where two colors are adjacent on a page; this compensates for mechanical press errors that can cause the two areas to spread apart, creating small gaps between the colors. Keeping these areas in precise registration is always a challenge for high-volume print runs (see Figure 3.16).

FIGURE 3.16 These two color areas are in close registration. They appear adjacent, with no gaps between the colors where the paper would show through.

Whenever two colors directly adjoin each other, there exists a possibility that they can become misregistered; you will see a gap between the two color areas where the paper underneath will show through (see Figure 3.17).

FIGURE 3.17 The same figure out of register.

Misregistrations can be caused by a number of factors, including paper stretch and shift, slight misalignments of the printing plates and rollers, or production errors. Misalignments of objects of even a few thousandths of an inch can cause misregistration problems on press.

To compensate for this possibility, production technicians intentionally overlap two color areas to create a trap. This allows for slight misregistration while keeping the two color areas adjacent (see Figures 3.18 and 3.19).

FIGURE 3.18 Adjacent colors can be "choked" and "spread" to create overlapping areas.

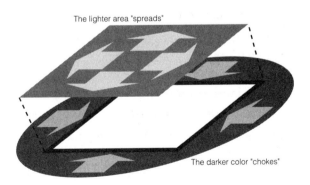

FIGURE 3.19 Colors "spread" out into adjacent areas, or "choke" into surrounded areas.

Trap (or **trapping**): The practice of overlapping adjacent color areas to compensate for slight misregistration.

Choke: The practice of shrinking the open interior area of one color object to overlap another color area that prints inside it.

Spread: The practice of enlarging an interior printed area to overlap the edges of a surrounding printed area.

How can you make sure that all of your color areas will trap correctly on press? There are two levels of intervention that you can perform to ensure proper trapping of your color areas.

Alternative 1: The Easy Way

In more complex documents, you may have a large number of potential problem areas such as innumerable imported EPS graphics, or continuous-tone full-color photographs with colored type areas knocking out of them. Tell your service bureau or printer that you've taken no action to change the document's trapping values, and that you'd like the bureau to make sure that everything traps properly. This puts the responsibility on their shoulders for correct trapping and registration.

There are a few high-caliber weapons that address this need. The Dolev PS2 is a hardware extension that adds this functionality to an existing Scitex scanning station. In contrast to a hardware-based solution, Aldus TrapWise and Island Graphics Island Trapper are two software-based products that run on common workstations to perform comparable functions.

These software-based products work by evaluating your document on the pixel level and determining which color areas require trapping and at what amount, based on the color density and intensity. Depending on what system your service bureau uses and what its individual trade practices are, this can increase your output costs by a factor of two or more, but the peace of mind and confidence in the work is more than worth the expense. At a 3380-pixel-per-inch resolution, there's a lot of data for this device to review.

Make sure that your service bureau has this capability. You wouldn't choose any but a fully equipped service bureau, would you?

Alternative 2: The Hands-on, More User-Intensive Way

If you are printing a document with a fairly uncomplicated page layout and fairly uncomplicated PostScript artwork throughout, you can trap all your graphic elements yourself. As with most things, it's simple if you know how.

In page-layout and composition programs like QuarkXPress, you can select and adjust color-trapping values on two levels; *globally*, meaning that every time the two edited colors appear next to each other they will trap a certain defined value that you set for the document, and *by item*, which means that individual items may be selected and have a custom trapping value applied to them.

For example, in order to globally change the trapping values of the two colors magenta and cyan in this QuarkXPress document, simply choose **Colors** under the Edit menu and select **magenta**. Then click the **Edit Trp** button and assign a new trapping value for any color that might appear next to magenta (see Figure 3.20).

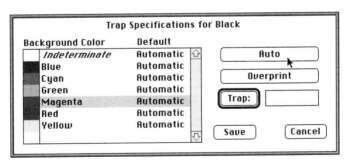

FIGURE 3.20 Assigning a trap value in QuarkXPress.

Adjusting a trapping value using the global method will affect all objects on a page that are assigned these colors—and at the value you've chosen.

This may cause problems, for example, if you're printing a large sheet with flat colors, and you've chosen a large absolute trapping value for your colors because you're anticipating a lot of paper stretch and shift due to the sheet size, be careful of smaller objects, such as type with serifs, that might close up with a large absolute trap defined (see Figure 3.21).

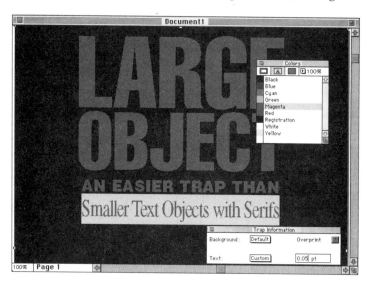

FIGURE 3.21 A large absolute trapping value will work fine to compensate for misregistration of large objects on the page, but watch out for small type, which might close up or otherwise distort in printing.

Local trapping in QuarkXPress is easy to apply. Simply select an object to trap, then choose **Show Trap Information** under the View menu to display a trap information palette (see Figure 3.22).

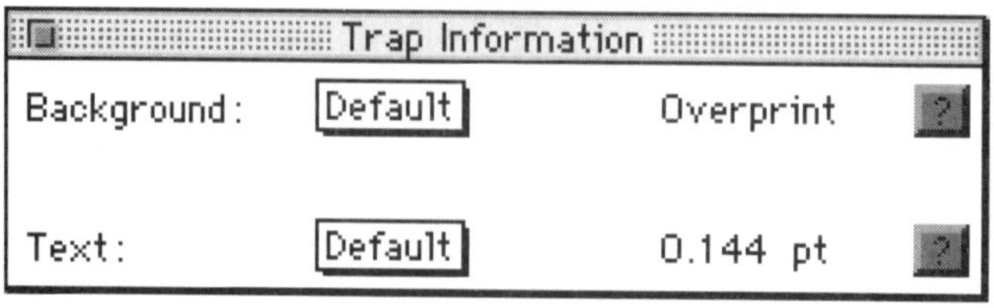

FIGURE 3.22 The Trap Information palette in QuarkXPress.

You can then select individual objects, such as type or line elements, and define a custom trapping value for them. This is a little more reliable than choosing to globally edit the trapping values, but a little more tedious in a document with a large number of trappable objects.

One situation where trapping cannot be accomplished within the page-layout software is in trapping PostScript artwork. Remember, PostScript artwork cannot be edited or changed within the page-layout software because the elements have already been assigned in the software that created them. Colors cannot be changed (as in grayscale or bitmapped TIFF or PICT images), and traps cannot be edited.

When creating PostScript artwork for production, you can create your own traps, chokes, and spreads by designating an overprinting border for your color areas. In this example we'll create a custom trap using the tools in Adobe Illustrator (see Figure 3.23).

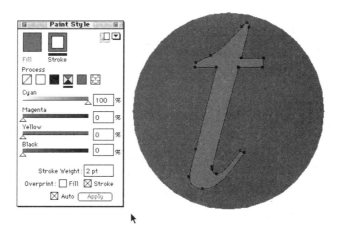

FIGURE 3.23 A custom trap in Adobe Illustrator.

The elements of this image must be trapped against one another by manually adding an outline stroke that will overprint the enclosed area. Here's how to do it yourself. Select the main area that must be trapped, and choose a stroke that is the same color as the surrounding area, in this case, cyan. After choosing the color, select the **overprint** option in the definition palette (see Figure 3.24).

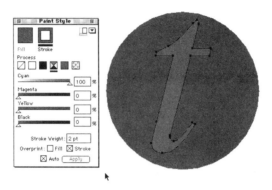

FIGURE 3.24 Since the interior of the object is a graduated color,
the exterior outline is chosen and made to overprint.

Remember that in drawing programs like Illustrator, the lines are measured from their centers, so choosing a 1-point line width will actually yield a 0.5-point overprinting trap (see Figure 3.25).

FIGURE 3.25 A 1-point line produces a half-point trap.

Because the objects, as they are created in Illustrator, are already defined and unchangeable outside of Illustrator, the outlines will be defined as overprinting in whatever page-layout software you are using. Now for the hard part. If the artwork is going to be reproduced at a different size from that at which you created it in Illustrator, be aware that any reduction or enlargement you apply in the page-layout software will affect the size of the overprinting trap areas you've created.

If you reduce the size of your image to 50% of the original size in your page-layout software, then the 0.5-point trap area you've designated in

Illustrator will become only a 0.25-point trap area, making a misregistration problem more likely, depending on the size and kind of press on which you're printing. Similarly, enlarging the same image to 400% of its original size will get you a trapped area of 2 points—unnecessarily large for most production techniques. Visually, this may not appear as professional as you'd like. When trapping your illustrations manually, take into account the size of your image as it is created and the size at which it will be reproduced (see Figures 3.26 and 3.27).

FIGURE 3.26 This image looks fine at the proper reproduction size.

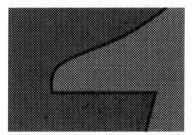

FIGURE 3.27 The same illustration enlarged 400%. Note the size of this trap!

Summary

Process color is a production method by which a printing press can simulate a much wider range of colors to create full-color photographic images or match specific colors using four basic process production colors.

To create four-color process production conventionally, images must be photo-mechanically separated, using sophisticated and expensive equipment and highly skilled technicians. Recent technological advances in the personal computer industry have brought these capabilities to the desktops of graphic designers and production artists in the form of scanners and software products such as Adobe Photoshop. Creating your own process color separations for production requires a little knowledge and the right software to fulfill most common production requirements.

Printers and production services use a technique called trapping to ensure that adjacent color areas will print in correct registration. In trapping, adjacent colors are overlapped slightly to compensate for paper shifting and stretching on the press as it is being printed. You can create and control trapping values in a document using the software tools on your computer.

While manual trapping of PostScript artwork is a possibility, your service bureau probably offers services that evaluate and adjust trapping in your digital documents. It's likely that the time you save will make up for any added expense involved.

Chapter 4

Hardware

* What kind of hardware performs which functions?
* What kind of hardware is needed for desktop prepress?

This chapter describes the minimum and optimum hardware requirements for the successful implementation of the concepts presented in this book. The text, flowcharts, and illustrations in this chapter will explain why the following equipment is necessary and what functions each component performs:

* the central processing unit, or CPU
* storage devices
* display devices
* proofing
* peripherals that can be added to your system

What Hardware Does What?

This section includes diagrams and roadmaps of a desktop prepress system, including possible workstation configurations and network and telecommunication topologies. The following issues will be discussed:

* when and why to upgrade hardware
* cost of hardware versus performance
* obsolescence

What Kind of Hardware You Need

It used to be much easier to be a graphic designer or illustrator. Most of what you did involved relatively simple tools like T squares and triangles, pencils and erasers, a drawing table, a lamp, a little wax, and an X-acto knife. You didn't have to know much about the tools; you just went down to your local art supply store and bought them by the handful.

While today's electronic tools provide a dizzying increase in speed and precision for the kinds of work that used to be done with simple mechanical tools, they also require us to know a great deal more about the tools themselves in order to make effective use of them. When the electronic design industry was new, the common complaint among designers was: "I'm a (insert one of the following: *designer, illustrator, art director, typographer, camera operator, production artist*), not a computer operator!" Resistance to change in this industry was strong but is fading as electronic design tools become more effective and the benefits of using them become increasingly obvious.

For example, using a simple X-acto knife did not require knowing the metallurgy or manufacturing processes that were used to create it. Nor did you need to know whether a particular knife was compatible with a certain brand of paper or wax in order to make use of it in your business. Tables were tables, knives were knives, and felt-tipped markers were felt-tipped markers.

Today, however, when considering the purchase of a workstation or desktop production system, the graphic designer is assailed with a confounding array of alternatives and choices of hardware and software with different capabilities and compatibilities—all of which affect the performance of every other element of the system. Tread carefully, learn slowly, and remember the words of Oscar Wilde: "Experience is the name everyone gives to their mistakes." Try not to get too much "experience" early in your career. You can avoid making at least some mistakes by "test-driving" each part of your system before purchasing it.

Don't be shy about asking for advice from your friendly neighborhood computer consultant. Seek out a consultant who has experience in the fields of graphic design and production. Don't expect the "helpful" assistant sales manager in the red vest and bow tie at your local computer superstore to know all the ins and outs of the graphic design and production business, much less how all the tiny details of how your microprocessor's bits and bytes, speeds and feeds will affect all the graphic design software you're about to purchase.

All of the components of your computer system—from the computer box itself to the monitor, printer, and network and storage devices—perform specific tasks in the process of helping you create and produce your work. This chapter will discuss each component's specific tasks and briefly describe how each component works.

The CPU

Let's start with the very center of all the activities that take place in your system: the *central processing unit*, or CPU. The CPU is the "brain" that controls all the other devices in your system. In the case of a desktop computer, the CPU takes the form of a large chip on the logic board inside your computer that controls all the other chips on the logic board. This is what gives the computer the power to perform millions of mathematical equations per second. This single complex chip—stronger than a pocket calculator, able to render tall buildings in a single bound—is the engine driving most of your system. This chip is what determines the character and personality of your computer.

The two most popular computer systems in the world today use two popular computing standards: RISC (reduced instruction set computing) or CISC (complex instruction set computing). High-performance computers using DOS-based Windows operating systems use the CISC-based Pentium processor, while newer Macintosh systems are based on Motorola's new RISC-based PowerPC processor. Both systems have their merits; however, industry experts and reviewers agree that the future of desktop computing will likely be in RISC-based processors. Since the competing processor platforms are running pretty much neck and neck speed-wise, the real benefit of any system is in efficiency of operation.

Apple's new Power Macintosh systems use the new PowerPC microprocessor and seem to hold the lead in processing speed for the moment. There are additional benefits and advantages in choosing Macintosh over Windows-based computers.

First, because Apple was the first to develop this market niche, the Macintosh has been the art community's standard for electronic graphic production. A good test of this point is to make a few telephone calls to local service bureaus to ask which file formats they prefer to image. Most will certainly claim to image files created on either platform; however, most will prefer Macintosh-created files because of all the inherent Macintosh system benefits. (By the way, this same test applies equally well when determining which brand of software to use to create your files. More on that later....)

Second, PowerPC chips consume less power than Pentium chips. Hence, they run cooler inside your system. Lower temperatures inside your computer's case allow your fan to work more efficiently and keep a cooler operating environment, causing less heat stress on all the other electronic components.

NOTE

On a level of corporate profitability, PowerPC chips are far cheaper to manufacture than Pentium chips (they are smaller, so more chips can fit on the silicon wafer disk from which they are manufactured). Apple, Motorola, and IBM have a better profit incentive to create machines that operate more efficiently and cost less to produce. In a competitive marketplace, these incentives weigh heavily in the consumer's favor.

Computers come in different configurations and form factors. There are small "pizza-box" models with few internal slots for expansion. These small computer cases usually house a logic board, a floppy disk drive, and a hard disk drive (and sometimes a CD-ROM drive).

Other computers offer the same performance, with more expansion and upgrade capabilities by allowing additional sockets on the logic board for plug-in expansion cards. These computers have larger cases to allow for at least three expansion cards.

Still other computers exist in a "tower" configuration with space inside the case for additional mass storage devices, such as extra hard disk drives, removable cartridges, or tape backup devices.

What is probably Apple's most significant contribution with RISC-based Power Macintosh computing is the computer's ability to seamlessly work with older, nonoptimized Macintosh applications. This means that a user who is upgrading from an older Macintosh to a new Power Macintosh will not have to worry about investing in all new software in order to take advantage of all the benefits of the new system. Older Macintosh software that was designed to run on Motorola's 6800-based CISC computing standard will run just as well on the Power Macintosh as it did on the old standard Macintosh.

The Hard Disk

Inside the case where the CPU resides, there is also a hard disk on which all the document information, application software, and operating system software are stored. Hard disks commonly hold between 20 megabytes and a gigabyte of information. Because the hard disk is inside your computer case, it draws its power from the internal power supply and is directly connected to your computer's logic board via an internal SCSI (small computer systems interface) connection.

When you wake up your computer in the morning, the first thing the CPU does is look for an internal hard disk on which the operating system is stored. The operating system controls the way the computer behaves and interacts with you and all of its peripherals (more on this later).

Hard disks with SCSI connections are also very fast in storing and retrieving information. The disk inside is spinning at a speed of thousands of revolutions per second, with a read/write head traveling laterally across the surface of the disk, magnetically reading and writing information on invisible "tracks" and "sectors." Hard disk capabilities are commonly described in milliseconds of average "seek time." When looking for a computer, keep in mind that a shorter seek time is generally better.

Be judicious in your considerations. If a $500 difference in price nets you a speed gain that can only be measured with an oscilloscope, you might be best served to save your rubles and get the marginally slower machine. In this case, your consideration should be toward the stability of the manufacturer and the strength of the machine's warranty.

Hard disks are connected to each other and to your computer using the industry-standard SCSI cables. SCSI is a fast and efficient standard that most manufacturers have embraced; it will most likely be in place for years to come. Currently, most computers will recognize only seven SCSI peripheral devices in a system. Each SCSI device has a unique single-digit "address" in the system (from 0 to 7) for the computer to identify it (see Figure 4.1). Conflicting SCSI addresses (two or more devices with the same SCSI address) in a system will cause problems, including system crashes and failures, but readily available shareware and a little knowledge can help you resolve these address conflicts.

FIGURE 4.1 A hard disk drive stores information magnetically on a very rapidly spinning disk, depositing and reading information in magnetic "roadmaps" that divide the disk into sectors and tracks.

The Floppy Drive

Most modern floppy diskettes are 3.5 inches in diameter and will hold 1.4 megabytes of information. Such diskettes are a popular medium because they are an industry standard. They fit in your shirt pocket, and each diskette holds a reasonable amount of information.

Macintosh computers will read and write to both Macintosh and DOS diskettes using a system extension called *PC Exchange*. There are also many third-party solutions available that provide the same functionality with a few added translation features. This means that any Macintosh computer with the correct system extension installed will be able to read, copy, and use files created on DOS systems. While many Macintosh programs are able to save their document files in a DOS-readable format, it is not always an easy task for a DOS machine to read Macintosh-formatted diskettes.

Other Internal Storage Options

Some computers can accommodate several different internal storage devices in addition to a hard drive and a floppy disk drive. Almost any external storage option can also be available as an internal storage solution. Mass storage devices mounted internally can take advantage of the computer's internal power supply and benefit from a direct SCSI connection to the logic board. Internal storage options include CD-ROM drives, additional hard disk drives, removable cartridge drives, and tape drives.

It is not uncommon to find the newer "multimedia" computers with an internal CD-ROM (compact disc–read only memory) drive mounted inside the main computer case. The main drawback to CD-ROM media is that they are read-only. You cannot save documents or change the data on CD-ROMs.

External Storage Devices

There are currently a wide variety of external storage options available. Each has different benefits and cost advantages. External storage devices have the basic advantage of being portable; they can be easily disconnected, transported, and reconnected to another system. In addition, they are a handy solution for people who have to transfer large volumes of data between different locations or between different systems in the same location.

CD-ROM Drives

External CD-ROM drives make CD-ROM media more portable between systems. CD-ROM is a very efficient storage medium since CD-ROM disks can hold large volumes of data (see Figure 4.2). Distribution of CD-ROM media has been increasing substantially in recent years and has become the preferred choice for multimedia publishers. The only caveat to CD-ROM media (besides the previously mentioned inability to write data to them) is that the drives are noticeably slower in reading data than standard hard drives or other removable media.

FIGURE 4.2 CD-ROM media are permanently inscribed to a reflective substrate surface using a laser beam. Another weaker laser beam is then used inside the CD-ROM drive to read the individual data bits as it is reflected from the surface material.

External Hard Drives

External hard disk drives offer the advantage of being very fast and portable storage solutions. Some external hard drives can hold several gigabytes of information in a small case. Before removable cartridge media were available, portable external hard drives were the most efficient way to transport large volumes of data.

Removable Cartridge Media

There are several removable cartridge systems available today that can hold impressive amounts of data and still offer respectable seek times and transportability. The most popular one now is a magnetic cartridge or "SyQuest" system that features removable hard disk cartridges that hold from 44 to 270 megabytes of information per disk (see Figure 4.3). Magnetic cartridge systems offer the benefits of being initially less-expensive hardware devices and having relatively fast cartridge access times. Read/write access times for magnetic cartridges rival those of standard hard disk drives, making storing and running application software from the cartridge instead of from an internal hard drive an attractive alternative.

FIGURE 4.3 Several types of magnetic media.

There are some drawbacks to magnetic cartridge systems, however. While the initial hardware expense is lower, the cost per megabyte of storage for the removable media is relatively high. There is also debate among drive manufacturers about the relative reliability of a totally magnetic cartridge. Information is stored on these cartridges the same way it is stored on regular hard-disk drives. But with removable cartridges, the danger of exposure to external magnetic fields—such as those surrounding television picture tubes, stereo speakers, and any electric motor—is greater, causing increased potential for data loss.

Magneto-Optical Cartridges

A relative newcomer to the storage scene is the magneto-optical cartridge system. Magneto-optical cartridges store their data in much the same way as magnetic cartridges. However, as their name indicates, magneto-optical cartridges offer the added reliability of being partially optical.

Magneto-optical cartridges are less susceptible to external magnetic fields and are more reliable for long-term archival storage. They also offer the benefit of having a convenient form factor with a lower cost per megabyte of storage. Magneto-optical cartridges come in 3.5-inch and 5.25-inch disk sizes with capacities ranging from 128 to 670 megabytes per disk.

Magneto-optical cartridges exhibit relatively slow access times. Seek-time speeds for reading information from a magneto-optical cartridge are comparable to speeds of other mass storage systems, but magneto-optical storage systems may run up to 30% slower than other cartridge systems when writing information to the disk. The write process requires three passes of the disk for writing and verifying the data on the cartridge.

Tape Drives

Another mass storage option is the tape drive. Tape cartridges can hold several gigabytes of information securely for archival purposes. They record and retrieve information serially, much the same way as your cassette deck at home does. Information is written and read sequentially from the beginning to the end of a tape.

Tape drives are an acceptable medium for archival storage of data, but they do not have a fast seek time because they are serial. The advantage of disks over tape is that information stored on a disk is easier and faster to find and retrieve than on a tape, which must read sequentially in order to access the data.

WORM Drives

WORM is an acronym for Write Once, Read Many. Data can be written to a worm drive only once but read from the cartridge as often and as many times as from any other medium. WORM drives are usually used as a permanent archival medium. Unlike CD-ROM, WORM media can be written to whenever necessary, until the cartridge's media capacity is reached. This type of storage system is ideal for situations where a design development trail may be audited after creation. Progressive updates to documentation or designs may be recorded, with each iteration becoming a permanent and unchangeable record.

The Monitor

The most visible part of your system will be your computer monitor or display. Monitors can be large or small and color or black and white. Prices of monitors range from reasonable to surprising.

There are three basic things to consider when purchasing a monitor: size, color depth, and pixel resolution. Monitors are measured diagonally across the screen from corner to corner; they commonly range from smaller portable displays of 7 to 9 inches to larger desktop displays of 21 inches.

Although a monitor's advertised size may be the diagonal measurement of the glass area of the picture tube, the actual viewable image area of a given monitor may be somewhat smaller. For example, the picture tube on a 21-inch monitor may measure 21 inches diagonally from corner to corner, but the image displayed on that tube may measure only 17 inches from corner to corner.

A monitor's color depth is an indication of how many colors it can simultaneously display. Monochrome monitors display no color at all; each pixel on the display will be black or white with no indication of grays or colors. Other monitors may display grayscale and color information and will be rated in terms of bit depth. Most monitors today are capable of displaying the entire spectrum of 16.7 million colors simultaneously, although some may require additional VRAM (video RAM) or additional cards to be installed in the computer's logic board to reach this bit depth.

Bit depth is a description of the number of possible colors that any single pixel can display. One-bit displays are monochromatic, showing only black or white pixels on the screen. On one-bit displays, gray colors are simulated by dithering the black and white pixels.

Some systems display only 256 simultaneous colors; these are referred to as "8-bit" displays. Grayscale images may be displayed as 8-bit, with the image being composed of 256 different shades of gray.

Most professional systems are configured to display 24 bits of color, or all 16.7 million colors in a computer's palette. To display this color depth on larger monitors, some systems require additional memory dedicated to video display, called VRAM. Some computers can accommodate the addition of VRAM directly to the logic board of the computer, while others may require the memory to be installed as part of an add-in NuBus card that assumes the job of color processing for the monitor.

Discuss your needs and capabilities with your local computer systems consultant or hardware vendor to determine what color depth monitor will work best for you.

Pixel density of computer monitors varies according to the model and system configuration. Macintosh computers have settled on a 72-pixel-per-inch display standard; each pixel is capable of displaying whatever depth of color the video output on your computer or add-in video card will support. This makes it convenient for users in the graphics world to see a relatively accurate representation on the screen of what they are creating at the object's actual size. Remember, the graphics world measures distances in points and picas, and there are 72 points per inch.

Some competing brands of computer displays support other pixel densities and can be configured by the user. While this may aid in displaying more pixels per inch, there are cases where this can lead to confusion and difficulties in actual versus displayed size.

Try comparing the ruler measurements on your computer's display in a few page layout programs (see Figure 4.4). Which ones come closest to true measurements?

T I P

FIGURE 4.4 Does your display measure up accurately?

Monitors display colors on the screen by mixing densities of red, green, and blue picture elements to visually simulate a range of colors (see Figure 4.5). Here is where a strange translation begins.

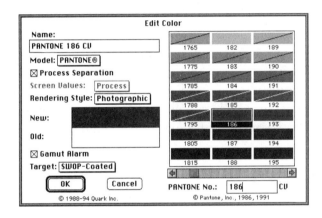

FIGURE 4.5 Selecting color.

Keep in mind that there are several color models to express various color imaging techniques and your system software and application software must work together to create an accurate translation between the various color models and what the monitor is capable of displaying. You may choose to display colors in your document's palette based on HSB (hue, saturation, and brightness), RGB (red, green, and blue), or the four process production colors, CMYK (cyan, magenta, yellow, and black). Your software will then instantly translate the colors into your chosen model for production art.

T I P

Because monitors, lighting conditions, and even your perception of color change subtly every moment, it is a good idea to have a color swatch book nearby to use as a reference. This will help to ensure that the colors you are choosing on screen are close to the colors that will print.

Large-screen displays are certainly the favorite of most computer designers. If you primarily work with standard 8.5- by 11-inch or smaller pages, and you typically work with more than one document open at a time, large screens are handy. They enable you to keep plenty of windows open, and they allow ample space for floating tool palettes.

Screen size becomes an issue when you begin to work with larger-format documents. If you are creating tabloid-size pages for production, or if your designs are for multipage spreads, then you might want to seriously consider the purchase of a 21-inch monitor to see as much of your work as possible on the screen.

If a large-format screen is not financially practical, you may want to consider purchasing a second smaller monitor. Macintosh computers can easily support multiple monitors via the Monitors control panel icon, with which you designate which will be your primary monitor. Your second monitor can then be available for extra open windows and tool palettes.

Input Devices

The Keyboard and Mouse

Your primary method for interacting with your computer will be with your keyboard and mouse. There are several styles of each available at reasonable prices. In fact, there are several competing input devices that are alternatives to a standard mouse.

Ergonomics should play a key role in your decision of which brand of keyboard and mouse to purchase. Unlike a casual user, you will be parked in front of your computer for extended periods of time, so you should consider ergonomics not just for comfort, but for your health as well.

Sit comfortably in your chair with your hands on your lap. Notice how your hands naturally point inward, not parallel to each other. Now hold your hands over a computer keyboard in the position in which you ordinarily work. Notice how a standard keyboard forces your hands into an unnatural position. Over time, this may become a painful annoyance and could lead to more serious injury, such as carpal tunnel syndrome.

If you are considering a third-party keyboard, however, you must make sure it is compatible with your computer system. Some keyboards require special software to be recognized by your computer. Check whether the keyboard you choose requires a special system extension or control panel in order for your computer to recognize it. This can be a problem when you upgrade your system software: Will the keyboard manufacturer be around to publish an update to its driver software? Another good thing to find out is the maximum number of keys that can be pressed for your computer to record a character. If your keyboard will only allow two keys to be recorded simultaneously, you may run into problems when using certain software products that have keyboard shortcuts using more than two keys (such as steering the spaceship in your favorite computer game).

Mouse Alternatives

Apple's single-button mouse is certainly a valuable contribution for simplicity in computer interfaces. You simply click, double-click, or drag to initiate commands and selections in your software. Some people have compared this to learning to draw with a garage-door opener. What could be easier?

There is no shortage of alternative pointing devices for the computer. These include trackballs, track pads, and pen stylus devices (see Figure 4.6). Most of these are reasonably priced and easily interchangeable, so don't be afraid to try several different types. If you can arrange a demonstration of any or all of these at your local computer reseller, you will be able to make a more informed try-before-you-buy choice; this may help you avoid committing to something of which you may grow tired in a short time.

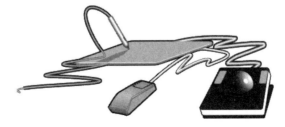

FIGURE 4.6 See how a comfortable, ergonomically designed keyboard allows your hands to rest more comfortably than a conventional keyboard.

A pen tablet seems to be the most expensive mouse option. Models with pressure-sensitive capabilities cost even more. Be aware, however, that the price of the device is not your only expense when purchasing this option. Pressure-sensitive pen input devices generally require additional RAM to operate, so be sure to take some time to try these devices and investigate all your options before committing your resources.

T I P

Keep your input devices clean. Purchase a can of compressed dry air and periodically blow out your keyboard and pointing device. Refer to your devices' owners' manual for instructions on how to disassemble and clean them. A clear way to demonstrate why this is necessary is to hold your keyboard upside down over a clean surface and shake it back and forth for a few seconds. You'll be surprised at what falls out.

Scanning Devices

Scanning technology continues to mature and become more affordable. With much of the same functionality as expensive and sophisticated drum scanners, desktop scanning devices convert optical images to digital information for use in your computer documents. Once converted, this information can be manipulated and output in a wide variety of formats and effects.

Scanned images continue to improve in quality and offer the designer and production artist more versatility in the final production of their work. For example, much of the image work that was performed by out-of-house service providers—including special stat camera, airbrush, and darkroom studios—may now be performed quickly, easily, and more cost-effectively on the desktop and then produced directly to film without engaging the services of a professional stripping department.

FIGURE 4.7 One obvious advantage to using scanned images in your page layout documents is the versatility with which you can adjust the output of your image. Each of the effects shown here would have required the use of outside services and would have involved unnecessary time and expense.

TIP

Scanners come with varying levels of dot-per-inch resolution capabilities. Some advertised high-resolution capabilities are actually an interpolated, or averaged, pixel resolution. Be wary of overstated claims made by scanner manufacturers. A good question to ask of your scanner manufacturer is, "Is that resolution claim actual or interpolated?"

Printing Devices

Inkjet Printers

Printers for your desktop system come in all sizes, resolutions, and capabilities. Depending on your production needs and budget, you can have camera-ready output on respectable black-and-white or color laser or inkjet printer. These printing and imaging devices cover the entire spectrum of quality and convenience. With a little expert advice, you can make an educated decision on which device will best suit your needs.

What used to be considered relatively high resolution is now considered a passable low-resolution proofing device. In this low-resolution arena there is a broad range of devices, from simple inkjet printers to more sophisticated laser printers.

Inkjet printers have a low initial hardware cost and relatively high per-page costs. Most inkjet printers are nonbuffered *serial* devices; that is, they do not support the SCSI communications standard, giving them a relatively slow printing speed. In most cases, they connect directly to your computer and cannot be easily shared across a network.

Most inkjet printers provide 360-dot-per-inch resolution, making them a great personal printing solution for the casual low-volume user. Standard inkjet printers are unable to interpret PostScript image code; instead, they print low-resolution screen-resolution snapshots of the PostScript images that appear on your computer's screen.

To their credit, inkjet printers connected to computers using a scalable font-rendering scheme, such as Apple's TrueType or Adobe Type Manager, create very clean fonts and few font-rendering problems (see Figure 4.8).

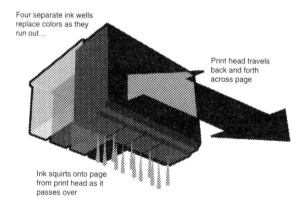

Four separate ink wells replace colors as they run out...

Print head travels back and forth across page

Ink squirts onto page from print head as it passes over

FIGURE 4.8 Inkjet printers work by squirting a jet of ink from a movable print head onto the paper as the print head moves back and forth across the page. Ink cartridges typically last for 200 to 500 pages, depending on the amount of ink coverage on each page. Because most inkjet printers have no memory or sophisticated processor inside, they are dependent on the computer's CPU and speed for their printing speed.

T I P

Some caveats to be aware of with inkjet printers:

* Slow print speeds: one-half to one page per minute depending on whether color or several different fonts are being used.

* Ink bleed: inkjet inks are water-soluble and will bleed if wet.

* Paper wrinkling: inkjet printer inks are applied wet, and extra care should be taken when *Best quality* is selected in the print dialog box. A page can get wrinkly even with average ink coverage. Make sure your pages are completely dry before stacking them.

Laser Printers

Laser printers are overwhelmingly the preferred proofing and printing medium for most computer users. Laser printers are a more cost-effective printing solution for medium-quality proofing and general better–than–letter quality capability. While the initial hardware cost is higher than for inkjet printers, the cost per page of output is much lower as you approach higher page volumes.

Every laser printer has its own internal CPU and memory on a logic board. This internal computer controls the imaging process, and the RAM memory affords a page image buffer. Most laser printers today offer 600 dots per inch resolution; just a few years ago only 300 dots per inch were possible.

Laser printers create images on the page by using a computer-controlled laser beam that changes the static charge of tiny dots on an imaging drum inside the printer. The drum rotates as the beam images each line of dots. Then a very fine dry powdered toner medium is attracted to those "exposed" areas of the imaging drum. As the drum continues to turn, it contacts the page, which has an opposite static charge, depositing the dry toner medium from the drum to the paper. The paper continues through the printing engine, passing under a hot corona wire heat source that fuses the toner onto the paper (see Figure 4.9).

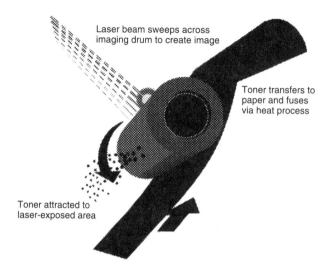

Laser beam sweeps across
imaging drum to create image

Toner transfers to
paper and fuses
via heat process

Toner attracted to
laser-exposed area

FIGURE 4.9 1. A thin laser beam controlled by the printer's internal CPU
creates an image on the toner drum. 2. The drum rotates and attracts a dry toner
to the image area. 3. The toner is then transferred to the paper as it contacts
the drum. 4. A corona wire heat source fuses the deposited toner to the paper.

A higher-quality smoother paper can make for a higher-quality image. Try different brands of specialty laser printer papers to see which works best for you.

Because the fusion of the laser toner medium to the paper is a heat-set process, it can create its own unique set of problems. Be careful about leaving your laser proofs in a high-temperature environment. Toner has been known to defuse and transfer from the paper to any adjacent contact medium, such as your car's dashboard or the inside of a vinyl notebook cover.

The same drawback works in favor of a special colorizing technique available from a few aftermarket suppliers. A few manufacturers sell devices that allow you to fuse special colors and foil effects to laser printer toners. Simply place the foil medium over the desired area of the laser-printed page, apply heat and pressure, and the foil or color medium will fuse to the toner. This makes for a great effect for short-run jobs, such as report covers or project proposals.

In a hurry? Do you not have enough time to order high-resolution camera-ready Linotronic output? For most quick-printed jobs, a 1270-dot-per-inch camera-ready resolution is acceptable. If you have a 600-dot-per-inch laser printer you can easily simulate a 1200-dot-per-inch resolution by printing your work at 200% of finished size and asking your printer to reduce the work by 50% to create your final camera-ready production artwork.

You can purchase laser printers that do not have a PostScript imaging capability. However, remember that most of the computer graphics world has standardized on PostScript as a page-description language, with PostScript drawing programs and PostScript-compatible fonts and page-layout programs. It's worth the added expense to have PostScript capability resident in your printer. Because laser printers have their own computers and logic boards controlling the imaging process, it is possible to upgrade a non-PostScript laser printer to a model with the PostScript language controller. This option is generally more expensive than purchasing the same printer with PostScript capability built in.

Color Printers

The cost of printing your own color proofs is dropping each year as the technology improves. Today, there are many cost-effective color printing techniques available. As laser printing technology has matured, so have the different color proofing techniques, each addressing different levels of quality, practicality, and cost-effectiveness.

Color thermal wax-transfer printers were among the first types of color printers to enter the desktop market. The wax-transfer process works by drawing one page of paper through the printer's mechanism and sequentially applying each of three process colors to the page via a heat-transfer process. Materials for thermal wax-transfer printers are relatively expensive, as they require a special color-transfer film roll. The film roll is actually an acetate carrier medium with sequential fields of cyan, magenta, and yellow. Each page that you image requires one pass of each of the colors, using up almost three feet of film for each page imaged (see Figure 4.10).

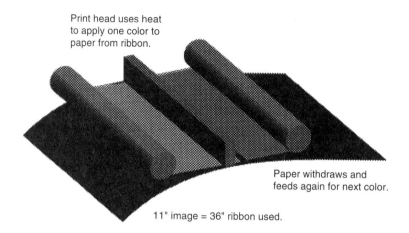

Print head uses heat to apply one color to paper from ribbon.

Paper withdraws and feeds again for next color.

11" image = 36" ribbon used.

FIGURE 4.10 Thermal wax-transfer printers are materials-intensive, using a relatively expensive color-transfer medium. The page must be drawn through and ejected from the device three times to create process colors. Each letter-sized image uses 36 inches of the acetate color ribbon.

To create each thermal wax-transfer image, each page is drawn through the mechanism to apply the first color, then ejected and drawn through again for each subsequent color. Thermal wax transfer provides an acceptable low-resolution color image whenever precise registration is not a requirement.

Color matching on thermal wax-transfer printers is a special challenge when creating images with dense halftones. As this is an additive color process, colors tend to become muddy with denser halftones.

T I P

Another popular color-printing process is color inkjet technology. Just as a black-and-white inkjet printer deposits ink on a page to create a sharp bit-mapped image, the color inkjet printer deposits all four process colors on a page using a special four-color print head. Color inkjet printers print at the same resolution as regular black-and-white inkjet printers, layering each of four translucent process colors on the page.

There are several drawbacks to color inkjet technology. It is a wet medium that takes time to dry and sometimes wrinkles the paper. In addition, the inks are generally water-soluble, making them unstable in humid environments. Color inkjet printers are generally slow, and most do not support PostScript.

When looking at color inkjet printers, consider one that has four separate process color cartridges instead of a single all-in-one cartridge. You may find it frustrating to replace a larger more expensive all-in-one cartridge each time you run out of black ink.

Dye-sublimation printers are perhaps the most dramatic of the color printer family. Dye-sub printers carry a high cost for hardware and materials, but they create striking color proofs using a heat and pressure process in concert with the same type of rolled acetate process-color carrier medium as thermal wax transfer. These printers use a thick RC paper similar to photographic paper. The color is impressed into the fiber of the paper itself through a heat and pressure process (see Figure 4.11). Because the color is sublimated into the paper itself, the full spectrum of colors is synthesized by mixing process colors together instead of simulating them through four-color process halftones.

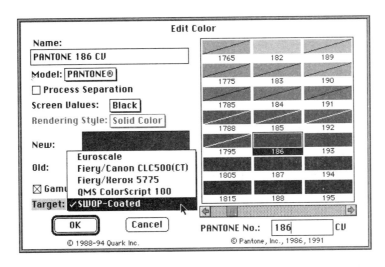

FIGURE 4.11 Dye-sublimation prints more closely simulate full-color photographs than process color halftones.

The color laser printer is an emerging and maturing technology for color imaging. Using the same type of dry toner-transfer technology as a laser printer to place a toner medium on paper, color laser printers create an image on a traveling belt instead of a drum to transfer four process colors of toner to paper. Some digital color copiers use the same technology as color laser printers and are becoming dual-use printing devices with the installation of a controller board that allows the computer to print images directly to the color copier.

Color laser printers require a very high initial investment in hardware. For the studio or service bureau that expects a high-volume color printing operation, they are a good cost-effective choice. Because they are digitally controlled through the computer, colors and color matching can be manipulated relatively easily for optimum quality output.

When deciding on your color-proofing device, remember that the final output will most often be four-color process offset printing. The most authoritative color proof is the one that most closely approximates the actual printing process itself. After creating a series of low-resolution color proofs for approval, your final color proof should be one that is made using the actual negatives generated for your final production. Ask your printer or service bureau to specify costs for a color match print or Chromalin proof using your final negatives to approve final color matching.

ColorSync and Color Matching Software

Now that you've got your full-sized color monitor and are viewing your documents in all their 24-bit color glory, and you are printing to your favorite cost-effective color proofing device, how do you know if these colors are accurate? Are the colors you see on-screen the real colors? They're different from the colors that came out of your printer. Is the printer printing accurate color? How can you tell?

There are a variety of color-matching systems available from a variety of manufacturers and publishers. Apple supplies its proprietary color-coordinating software, ColorSync, with all its color-capable devices. Quark ships a version of EFI's EFIColor software with its flagship product,

QuarkXPress. Even Kodak, the developers of PhotoCD , have a proprietary color-management software: KCMS.

These products attempt to match up a variety of color-producing and color-displaying devices so that you get predictable output from your software more often. Most color-management products work by providing a color "profile" of each color printing device, which the color-management utility interprets and translates into a more closely matched image on-screen. A device's color profile contains information on what colors that device is capable of printing and then adjusts the displayed color to match, making the screen preview of the color closer to the actual printed color.

For example, if you are using QuarkXPress and you have the EFIColor option enabled, your final output may be sheet-fed web-offset process (SWOP) color, meaning that the final product will be printed on some form of offset press using process colors. To designate this, you would choose **SWOP coated** as your target device in the color selection dialog box. Notice how certain colors in the Pantone color palette have lines through them diagonally, indicating that these colors will not reproduce faithfully with the selected printer device.

If you are using a color-management software product and do not have a corresponding color profile for your printer, contact your printer's manufacturer and/or the color-management software's publisher. At least one of them should be able to provide the appropriate color profile at a reasonable price.

What is a Network?

Before computers pervaded the design studio, networking generally meant one thing: exchanging information with others in your field, usually over lunch or cocktails or after hours in trade groups and associations. That meaning is still valid, although the tools we use now are considerably more complex.

The term *networking* still pertains to the exchange of information, but now it mostly means the exchange of information between computer workstations. The information that passes between computers may be documents and files transmitted from the computer to the printing device or anything else contained on a shared computer's hard drive.

How Does It Work?

Computers are connected to each other with a special wire or cable through which the information is sent. Unlike telephone services, in which there is a common standard for transmission and connection throughout the United States, there are several competing (and complementary) network products, each offering different levels of capability and *bandwidth* volume. Bandwidth refers to the amount of information and the speed at which it is transmitted. A broader bandwidth is capable of exchanging a larger volume of information in less time.

The simplest network to understand is no network at all, commonly referred to as *SneakerNet*. If you want to share and exchange information between nonconnected computers, you can copy your data to a floppy disk and hand-carry it to the receiving computer.

If you wanted to send larger files at higher speeds across longer distances, you could copy your large files to several diskettes, put on your best running shoes (or sneakers), and sprint across the building to deliver your information... hence the term "SneakerNet."

Now, of course, there are several schemes for exchanging information between computers. The easiest to use is AppleTalk, which is built into every Macintosh computer. Even Apple's lowest, oldest, and slowest computers are AppleTalk-capable. With AppleTalk you can connect up to 25 Macintosh computers either directly to each other or through a shared printer to send and receive files between all computers using Apple's simple drag-and-drop Finder metaphor. AppleTalk's main advantage is its inclusion with every Macintosh. Its main drawback is its slowness in transferring larger files across the network.

That's right, folks. The ability to connect computers to each other, share information, and print to shared devices is built into every Macintosh (at no additional cost or obligation), and always has been.

Prepare to Share

In order to use AppleTalk to share files between two Macintosh computers, there are a few steps to start the process.

> This initial setup procedure is not automatically enabled when you first start up your Macintosh because sharing demands some processing resources that are not necessary for nonshared devices. Once you establish sharing for your computer, it remains enabled and active until you turn it off.

First, make sure that both computers are connected, either directly through one of your serial ports or through a sharable printing device such as an Apple LaserWriter. Make sure both computers are turned on. You'll need to perform the following steps on both computers.

1. In order to activate AppleTalk, first select the **Chooser** in your Apple menu.

2. When the Chooser opens, activate AppleTalk by clicking the **Active** radio button at the bottom of the window. Then close the Chooser.

3. Select the main hard drive icon on your desktop and choose **Sharing** under your File menu.

   The system will present a dialog box telling you that you cannot share files until you activate sharing capabilities with the Sharing Setup control panel in the Control Panels folder. You'll need to perform a few other functions there as well. Click **OK**.

4. In the Sharing Setup control panel, click the **Start** button to activate file sharing. If you want to require a password for access security, do that here also. The system will require a moment to activate file sharing.

   You are almost there. The basic capability is now in effect. You can now assign certain access privileges with the Users & Groups control panel. To do this, choose **Control Panels** from the Apple menu.

5. In order to allow others to connect as guests to your machine with the access privileges you've assigned, double-click the **Guest** icon and click the checkbox to allow guests to connect to your machine.

Remember, AppleTalk is comparatively slow for network traffic. Unless you're using a very high-speed transmission medium, such as Ethernet, and unless you have a sophisticated server system established, it's probably a good idea *not* to check the **Program Linking** option.

After you've set up sharing on all the machines you intend to connect, your housekeeping chores are pretty much finished for now. Your machines are prepared to be connected.

Access to Other Machines on Your Network

Once you've prepared your machines to be connected to each other, you must make the actual connection. Open the **Chooser** again. Note that the indication at the lower-right corner of the window shows that AppleTalk is active.

Choose the **AppleShare** icon in the Chooser window to see which sharable machines are available to you You can choose any of these by double-clicking on its name in the window or by selecting it and clicking **OK**.

Then you will be able to select the other machine (or any of its connected volumes) and choose to automate the connection process each time your machine starts up. For now, just select the desired machine and click **OK**. As if by magic, an icon representing your connected machine will appear on your desktop.

You can open this icon, view its contents, or copy files to and from it (assuming you have designated the appropriate access privileges) using Apple's drag-and-drop or copy and paste techniques. It is very quick and easy.

Best of all, this capability (and profound convenience) is built right into every Macintosh computer. No extra software to buy, no extra cards to install, no huge installation hassles. It's all right there in every Macintosh. Sharing files between machines is as simple as dragging their icons back and forth. No more SneakerNet (even though the exercise is probably good for you).

One other great benefit to networking your computers is a little-known feature of Apple's operating system called "Publish and Subscribe." If you are using System 7 or later and are sharing files over a network, you can use Publish and Subscribe to keep all your imported image documents current in your page-layout program without having to manually reimport updated data. It works like this: After importing image data to your page-layout software, choose **Subscribe to...** under the Edit menu and select the original image document by navigating the menu that appears.

Then select **Subscriber Options...** under the Edit menu to define when and how this image will automatically update.

This is especially useful if you are importing art that is being created and edited on another workstation and that may be changed several times in the course of completing a project. Each time you open your page-layout document, it will automatically search on the network and check to see if the images imported from other workstations have been changed. If they have, they are automatically reimported with all the new changes. What a convenient enhancement to the file-sharing capability, and it's built in to every Macintosh.

Big Bandwidth

AppleTalk is a wonderful convenience. It is inexpensive, and it comes with every Macintosh. The one and only AppleTalk caveat is its transmission speed. Large files can take a while to transfer across the network. It's a lot like trying to drain the contents of a tanker truck with an ordinary garden hose. A larger hose or a faster pump would save time.

Ethernet is an alternative connection scheme that offers higher transmission bandwidth (faster speeds, larger volume). It requires special cabling and additional software, but the Ethernet connection capability is built into most of Apple's newer Macintosh computers.

AppleShare works the same over EtherNet as it does over AppleTalk. You'll go through the same setup procedures, and it will operate the same way, only much faster. This can be a real productivity enhancer as files travel faster over an EtherNet network. If you're working in a high-volume shop or sending large files across your network, then Ethernet is definitely the way to go.

Ethernet comes in a few different flavors and cabling schemes. Depending on your usage, how your office is prewired for other network services, and what your growth plans are, you should probably consult with your systems consultant or information services department about which scheme will work best for you.

Servers with a Smile

As your network and system grow to accommodate a larger volume of work, it may make sense to have a central storage place to keep commonly used items, including applications, fonts, and files. For example, if you're keeping 25 megabytes of fonts on every machine in your organization, your resources might be more efficiently used by keeping the same 25 megabytes of fonts in a single accessible location, making them available on demand to each workstation as needed, thereby freeing up hard disk space on all the workstations for other uses.

Thus is the concept behind the *server*. A server acts as a central storage place for your data, accessible by all the connected workstations on the network, holding files, applications, fonts, or anything else that needs to be stored. If you picture your workstation's hard drive as a filing cabinet, then a server might be a warehouse, with forklifts transporting your data to and from storage areas, serving your network's needs.

A server does not have to have an overly huge hard drive to be useful (although like money, MTV1, and RAM, too much is never enough). You can assign your server to act as a print server whose only purpose is to temporarily hold files being imaged to a printing device. When the user is finished working on a project, instead of being directly sent to the printer, thereby congesting network traffic, the file is sent to the print server— which then takes care of all the printing chores. This alleviates network traffic and allows you, the user, to get back to productive work without further interruption or delay.

Summary

Networking is a way to connect workstations and printers together to share information like files, fonts, and applications. The ability to connect computers and to share information and devices is included with every Macintosh in the Macintosh operating system using AppleTalk and AppleShare. Faster networking solutions are available, using EtherNet as the communications standard. These systems offer faster transmission times and broader bandwidth for more efficient communication between workstations.

File sharing also provides the ability to handle a server, a central storage place for projects, fonts, and applications. This frees up workstation resources. Servers can also automate and perform tasks such as printing, alleviating network traffic and processor resources.

Chapter 5

Software

- ❋ Operating systems
- ❋ What types of software you need, what softwares do, and why you need them
- ❋ Summary

Operating Systems

Much of what gives any computer its overall character and personality; what allows you to interact with it, give it commands, and see the results of your work is found in your computer's operating system. For years, there has been a battle of operating systems in the computer industry between Apple's user-friendly Macintosh operating system, which runs only on Macintosh computers, and Microsoft's Windows operating system, which is designed to run on any DOS-based computer.

Apple's proprietary operating system comes free with every Apple computer sold. It is a vastly more efficient operating system than Windows. It allows your system to use more of its processing horsepower for application tasks such as image processing and page layout instead of basic operating tasks like handling files, directories, fonts, sounds, and images. The capability to handle sounds and display floating palettes, windows, and graphics is built into the operating system, unlike Windows, which is a layer on top of the computer's DOS operating system.

On top of that, Macintosh computers are designed from the ground up to be immediately connectable to a wide variety of peripherals and to each other. For example, the series of steps involved in connecting a new hard disk drive to an Apple system is relatively short and easy. You simply install the device's driver software into your System folder by dragging its icon from the floppy disk onto the icon for your System folder, then plug the device's SCSI cable into the corresponding SCSI port on the back of your Macintosh. When you restart your Macintosh, the icon for your external hard disk will be on your desktop. Furthermore, if you would like to connect more devices to your Macintosh, the process is this short and simple for each device.

The steps involved in accomplishing the same task in the Windows environment are substantially more complex, requiring you to open your computer, set dip switches, install driver cards and software, make changes in your **WIN.INI** file with a text editor, and hope the cards, devices, and software do not cause any conflicts with the rest of your system and peripherals. So-called compatible peripherals actually require incredible effort to make the system recognize and use them.

Since there are no standards in the DOS world, manufacturers and publishers have no obligation or incentive to make sure that their devices are compatible with others. Remember, you are not working in a vacuum where all your work is drawn to you. You are competing with other designers and studios who are using Macintosh computers. If it takes them five minutes to install a new device and it takes you half a day to do the same task (and there are so many other tasks just like this), who do you think will have more time to take the client to lunch (or complete the work or do more client prospecting)?

While popularly perceived as having a lower hardware cost, computers capable of running Microsoft's Windows operating system actually end up being more costly solutions. Given that there are no standards in effect, the system software is inconsistent and harder to use across different applications (requiring more time for training and maintenance), and comparable systems with comparable performance and capabilities actually cost more and deliver less value. It is easy to see why the Macintosh system is a better choice.

TIP

If you're in a situation where you have to decide between these competing systems, you owe it to yourself to directly compare any two similar desktop systems side by side in order to make an intelligent choice of which to purchase. Set up an appointment with your local computer reseller and place comparably configured desktop graphics systems next to each other. Get out your stopwatch and record the amount of time it takes to remove a font from the system or to change the amount of memory a given program will use when running. It will be easier to make your decision if you have some hands-on experience from which to draw your own conclusions. All the glossy brochures in the world cannot convey the true essence of any computer.

It used to be an "either-or" world. Users had to choose one system over the other and forget about working in the other world. In recent years, however, the barriers between the platforms have been receding. Macintosh computers have long since been able to read and write to DOS/Windows diskettes. Today, you can even purchase Macintosh computers that will run both the Macintosh and Windows operating systems simultaneously. You can cut and paste information between both systems running on the same computer. The one caveat to this capability is that Windows applications occupy much more space on a hard disk drive than Macintosh applications, so if you're prepared to use a system with these capabilities, be sure to have a hard disk with enough storage capacity to accommodate the added space requirements.

Choosing a workable system for your studio today requires consideration of several important factors, outside of the obvious "How much?" and "How fast?" Here are some valuable tips for you to consider when deciding what your studio system is going to look like and what services you will offer.

Knowing what you know now, you can make a more informed decision on which type of computer system to purchase, which peripherals are an immediate necessity, and which may be upgraded at a later date, and most importantly, the potential profitability over time of your intended purchase.

One of the remarkable features of any Macintosh system is that the lowest slowest system Apple makes will run all of the advanced software you can purchase. For example, monochrome systems can work with and manipulate color software products, even though you cannot view the color changes on-screen. The question then remains: How fast (or slow) can you tolerate your system's performance? If you can live with a system that seems to crawl along at a glacial pace, allowing you a few relaxing "coffee moments" between operations while your computer processes your work and refreshes the screen, then consider the purchase of a not-so-lightning-fast Macintosh system.

However, be aware that the pause between operations that you were certain you could live with comfortably while you were reviewing the sales department's invoice will become intolerable as soon as you find yourself in any kind of a deadline situation.

You might also consider the amount of time you'll be required to spend maintaining your system. If you're spending a significant amount of your time installing fonts, managing your local area network, and configuring software and memory requirements, it will soon become clear that a simpler and more powerful system makes more sense for your business.

A system that works will pay for itself much faster than one that doesn't. However, a system that works fast will not only pay for itself but will also generate handy profits that you will most certainly feel compelled to spend on even faster computer equipment. So begins your new awareness of and addiction to processor speed. This consumer dependence on performance is what computer manufacturers build their business growth models on.

Concept: The Portable Production Artist

If your career path finds you serving the creative community as a freelance production artist, or even if you're in a salaried staff position and you find yourself always having to trade offices with account representatives, then here's a workable employment concept for you to consider.

With Apple's new family of Macintosh PowerBook portable notebook computers, a talented art director, designer, or production artist can become a totally portable fully-equipped freelance art studio. With a portable computer system, the designer or production artist can work anywhere, produce and deliver assignments on disk or via electronic network, and then bill the host studio via an internal fax modem or the host studio's laser printer.

Here's how a system like this might look: Start with a Macintosh PowerBook with plenty of dynamic RAM (DRAM) and a color display. Add whatever portable peripherals you feel are necessary (perhaps an external pointing device such as a pen stylus or mouse to augment the PowerBook's trackpad). Make sure your PowerBook holds all the appropriate software products to perform your work (in compliance with all applicable copyright laws) and includes a fast modem with fax capabilities. You might also want to consider carrying a few extra cables to connect your system to your client's local network, external hard disk drives, or even any convenient RJ-11 telephone jack. With Apple's Remote Access software, you can easily connect to your desktop system at home to retrieve any needed files.

Arrive on time for your assignments; exhibit remarkable creativity, talent, and craftsmanship; produce a high-quality and satisfying product for your client; print a convenient invoice that affords you a reasonable profit and pays for your computer system, your rent, and a luxurious vacation in Hawaii.

Portable production artists carry in their briefcases all the functionality and convenience of a full desktop system. This enables them to provide all the services that used to tie them to a drawing table or office studio (see Figure 5.1).

FIGURE 5.1 Splash screens from PageMaker and QuarkXPress.

Software

* ❋ What type(s) you need
* ❋ What each type does
* ❋ Why you need software

No discussion of graphic design and production on the desktop is complete without consideration of the most important element of your system: software. Software is the fuel that drives the electronic engine that you've chosen to propel you to your career goals. Just as NASA's space shuttle is a large, complex, expensive, and useless tribute to technology without a special mix of liquid hydrogen, oxygen, and a pair of solid rocket boosters, even the fastest, most powerful, sleekly packaged computer system will not do much for anyone without software to run on it.

The fact is, your career depends on being able to perform your job reliably, quickly, and accurately—and a system and software combination that affords unwelcome surprises can't help but negatively affect your ability to provide the best service possible to your clients. Choosing the right software products for the job will have a direct and immediate effect on your bottom-line profitability.

This chapter describes a basic, functional, and reliable software collection to which you can add your own bells and whistles to enhance your working experience. All of the following product descriptions illustrate capabilities and do not necessarily endorse any one product or family of products. Wherever competing products are listed as providing similar capabilities, a brief overview of those products' key features are given for comparison.

Remember, the best test of any product is the experience of its users. If you have any questions about advertised claims or reliability of a particular product for your uses, don't be shy about asking your silent partner in this business, the service bureau operator. Chances are that if you're considering using any software product for your computer, your service bureau operator has already had extensive (and expensive) experience with it, either by direct use or through the experience of some of their other clients.

It's in your service bureau operator's best interests to work with products that run reliably and quickly. Every time the regular flow of production is interrupted, by a failure of either the system or a software program, the bottom line is affected. To the service bureau operator, a smooth workflow is essential to maintaining a viable business. So it's likely that your service bureau operator will have some useful opinions on which software products live up to the claims of their publishers.

Make friends with your service bureau operator, as you and your service bureau will be working closely together. Rely on the operator's judgment and advice to help you create accurate and reliable production art.

TIP

Fortunately, an allegiance to one brand of products over another is not the issue that it once was. File formats are easily compatible between applications and accommodate a variety of capability requirements and computer platforms (some more than others; more specifics on that later). For example, one of the most common high-resolution file formats, EPS (encapsulated PostScript), is readily transferable across both Macintosh and Windows platforms with all the benefits of PostScript images present on both machine families.

Software Essentials

Which software products do you need to do your best work? Which products perform as advertised? And, more importantly, which products are more likely to cause problems and unexpected results? This section discusses a basic foundation of software products you'll need for desktop publishing.

Operating System: Maintenance and Management

First, of course, is the operating system. If you're using a Macintosh computer, then the software that runs the system, finds the files, builds the windows, and creates all those handy little pull-down menus is already present and almost invisible to you. It comes with every Macintosh and is included free with your purchase of the computer. The important point about your operating system is that the easier it is to understand and use, the easier it will be for you to perform basic operating system maintenance and management, including installing and removing fonts, sounds, and system extensions and changing memory requirements for your applications. With Macintosh it is as easy as dragging icons into the appropriate folders.

Page-Layout Software

Page-layout software "puts it all together" by combining graphic images and text on the same page. Whether the primary use of your computer will be precise technical renderings, photographic image manipulation, typography, three-dimensional renderings, or digital paintings, putting all your work into a single document for printing will require a page-layout software package such as PageMaker or QuarkXPress. Page-layout software affords you precision and flexibility in combining pictures and text on a page, great precision in the control and manipulation of type, and convenience and cost savings in camera-ready production.

The two major contenders for market share in the page-layout product field are PageMaker and QuarkXPress. Both offer remarkable precision and control over both type and images, both support third-party additions to the programs to add functionality, and both are trying hard to bill themselves as the *de facto* standard application in use for desktop publishing and layout. The argument over which is better will likely continue as long as each has their own in-house marketing department to write their press releases.

Feature Wars

Ever since the Macintosh and the first LaserWriter printers revolutionized the graphics design and production industry, there has been competition between the main vendors to produce a better, more efficient, more precise, and more comprehensive page-layout software product. Each vendor has added many features and capabilities until each has become a huge, memory-hungry (but immensely capable) graphics production tool. Now it's possible to compose pages with remarkable precision and automate the output process to suit any production needs.

While the competition between the two products' marketing departments continues to escalate the feature wars, a comprehensive table of comparable features can be obtained from the respective publishers, highlighting each product's relative advantages over the competition (as seen by the marketing department). Features offering significant advantages over other products are few and far between. Some that are of importance to you might be in the areas of precision and document construction.

One-thousandth of a point or one em-space may not seem significant to you until you need to align two adjacent process-color objects against each other—and the difference in location of a single row of halftone dots can give the impression of an object being out of registration, nonparallel, or uneven. This level of precision is imperative.

In addition, the ability to compose documents in a graphical fashion by dragging thumbnail images of their pages may seem like an unnecessary feature until you try it once and see how much time is saved in constructing a 200-page catalog.

QuarkXPress

QuarkXPress is the *de facto* standard page-layout tool among graphic design and production professionals. Just ask Quark. It boasts accuracy and precision to within .001 (1/1000) of any unit of measure; it automatically separates process and spot colors for prepress production; and it has an extensive collection of third-party filters (or Xtensions) that add a remarkable spectrum of functionality to the program.

Quark's Metaphor

QuarkXPress uses a "box" metaphor as a system for composing pages. In simple terms, this means that everything you create or import within QuarkXPress must be contained in a "box" or "item" that you create using the tools in the tool palette. Boxes may be any shape or size and have individual attributes such as transparency, border width, and background color. There are two basic types of boxes: those that contain text and those that contain graphics.

QuarkXPress's Greatest Hits

QuarkXpress's main claim to fame is its typographical control. Text can be kerned and tracked to within 5/10,000 of a point; leading may be specified to within 1/1000 of a point; and text may be compressed or extended from 25% of original width to 400% of original width in 1% increments. In addition to all this, QuarkXPress supports automatic drop caps and a surprisingly useful paragraph rule capability, making professional typography and great typographical effects easy tasks to accomplish within the program (see Figure 5.2)

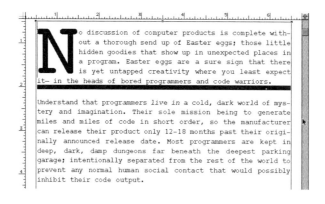

FIGURE 5.2 Automatic drop caps in QuarkXPress.

The Floating Palettes of Taipei

QuarkXPress uses a system of floating palettes to control much of what you do within the program. Palettes allow you to manipulate items and their contents with great precision. Palettes exist as a shortcut to many of the menu commands and keyboard shortcuts found throughout the program. For example, the process by which you would change the leading in a paragraph can be executed in any of three ways:

1. Via the measurements palette with a click of the mouse (see Figure 5.3).

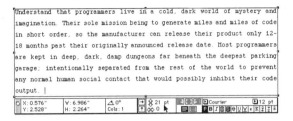

FIGURE 5.3 Leading inserted with the mouse.

2. Defined, by selecting the appropriate field in the Measurements palette, or via a simple menu command (see Figure 5.4).

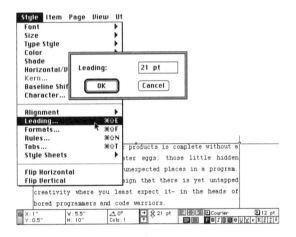

FIGURE 5.4 Leading inserted by value.

3. Incrementally using the keyboard shortcut **Command-Shift-Option:** or ' (see Figure 5.5).

FIGURE 5.5 Leading inserted by keyboard command.

QuarkXPress has a number of other palettes. The Document Layout palette for creating master pages and rearranging the order of pages in a simple graphical interface (see Figure 5.6).

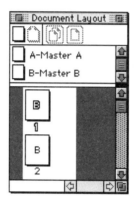

FIGURE 5.6 Quark's document layout palette.

The Colors palette is for specifying colors and color tints for borders, text, pictures, and backgrounds, including a clever array of color blends (see Figures 5.7 and 5.8a-f).

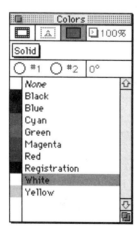

FIGURE 5.7 The Colors palette.

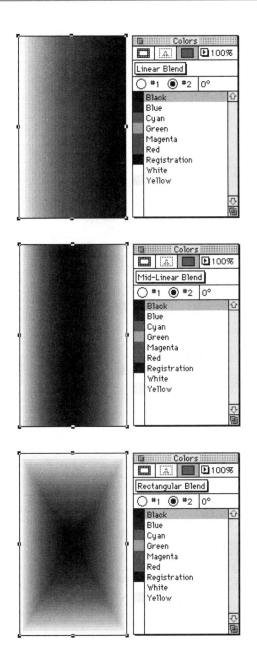

FIGURES 5.8a-c Different blends available in QuarkXPress.

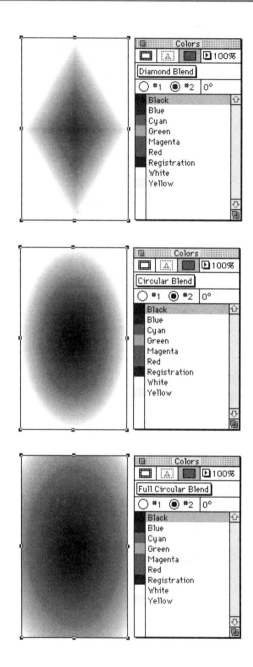

FIGURES 5.8d-f Different blends available in QuarkXPress (continued).

The Style Sheets palette allows you to change and manipulate text style sheets with a simple mouse click (see Figure 5.9).

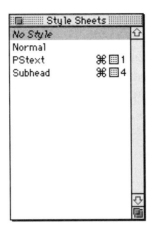

FIGURE 5.9 The Style Sheets palette.

The Trap Information palette not only shows vital trapping information about your selected objects but also allows you to change trapping values for selected objects (see Figure 5.10).

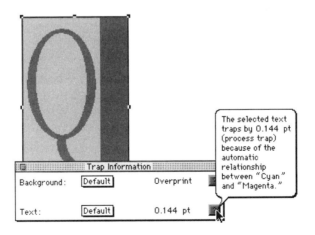

FIGURE 5.10 The Trap Information palette.

Welcome to Xtension Land

While QuarkXPress is a versatile, precise, and comprehensive page-layout tool, there are some specialized needs that it does not address. These include the ability to automatically lay out pages in a form for creating booklets and the ability to automatically create complex crossword puzzles. Luckily for the users who need this added functionality, there is a diverse collection of third-party filters and Xtensions to address these needs.

Created by companies and individuals outside of Quark, these Xtensions address specialized applications and environments from magazine layout to large-format newspaper production. They also enhance existing features found within the program and automate many functions. Third-party Xtensions are available through an independent company called XChange. They can be reached at (800) 788-7557.

If you want to create your own Xtensions, it is relatively easy to do. It requires a knowledge of the C programming language and a little help from the third-party product relations department at Quark (see Figure 5.12). They will even help you market your Xtensions to Quark users through the XChange catalog.

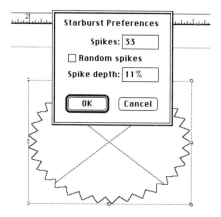

FIGURE 5.11 Third party XTensions are widely available.

Another source of useful Quark XTensions is Quark itself, which publishes a select collection of free Xtensions with every new version of QuarkXPress.

These collections began in 1991, starting with the simple **Bob**. Next came **Son of Bob** and **Bobzilla**. If you don't already own any of the free Quark Xtensions, place a call to Quark and ask for the current Freebies diskette, or download them from your favorite online service.

QPS

QuarkXPress is not a one-trick pony. Quark has also produced an exceptional new product called the Quark Publishing System, or QPS. QPS is, in essence, a tool for creating the virtual composing room. It allows staff working at remote locations to contribute to and create complete layouts for production without having to be in the same room.

QPS works by electronically linking writers, composers, editors, and artists to create a common layout. Writers assigned to specific stories can work on the layout, seeing how type and graphic page elements are working together. Editors can see and direct progress for each section as it is completed with messages that are transmitted across the network. Imagine a virtual workplace, where writers, artists, and editors never actually meet. They can work in their separate homes, in cities thousands of miles apart. Taking the concept a step further, with wireless modems and a global access network, a worker might not even need to be anywhere near a city, telephone, or power supply to complete an assignment. Beaches, ski slopes, mountain tops, and treehouses can become the perfect work environments!

You can reach Quark, Inc. at (800) 788-7835 for more information.

PageMaker

PageMaker is the de facto standard page-layout tool among graphic design and production professionals. Just ask the Adobe Corporation (formerly Aldus).

With a system of floating palettes similar to that of QuarkXPress, PageMaker accomplishes much of what QuarkXPress can do on a page with similar precision and control. The most obvious differences are in the document construction procedures. PageMaker allows only two master pages (right side and left side of the same document) per document—compared to 127 in QuarkXPress. There are other dissimilarities in the areas of text control and editing, as well as in color control and separation of colors—specifically, automatically trapping of colors in production.

To its credit, PageMaker also offers as large a variety of third-party filters as QuarkXPress does. PageMaker's extensions are called *Additions*; they provide new functionality and features that address special uses and markets.

TIP Contact the Adobe Corporation for more information about PageMaker Additions and a full description of features. You can reach the company at (800) 333-2538.

Other Page-Layout Programs

There are a host of alternatives to QuarkXPress and PageMaker that offer similar features and capabilities at a comparable price. Before deciding which page-layout product is right for you, check with your service bureau to see if it supports that software, and if it does, what its experiences with the product have been. Count on the service bureau to make a credible recommendation.

With the incredible success of programs like QuarkXPress and PageMaker, there have been more than a few competitors seeking to exploit this lucrative market segment. Filling niches that require a less comprehensive feature set, less complexity, and smaller memory requirements, these products have grown to specialize in single-page and short-run documents.

Great Work, Great Efforts

With the right arsenal of special tricks and techniques, a skillful user of PageMaker or QuarkXPress can create and produce remarkable printed work with this software (see Figure 5.12). There are hundreds of useful and creative user tricks that can be accomplished with both programs.

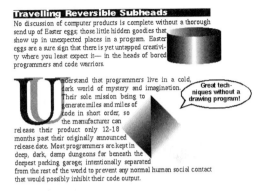

Travelling Reversible Subheads

No discussion of computer products is complete without a thorough send up of Easter eggs; those little hidden goodies that show up in unexpected places in a program. Easter eggs are a sure sign that there is yet untapped creativity where you least expect it— in the heads of bored programmers and code warriors.

Understand that programmers live in a cold, dark world of mystery and imagination. Their sole mission being to generate miles and miles of code in short order, so the manufacturer can release their product only 12-18 months past their originally announced release date. Most programmers are kept in deep, dark, damp dungeons far beneath the deepest parking garage; intentionally separated from the rest of the world to prevent any normal human social contact that would possibly inhibit their code output.

Great techniques without a drawing program!

FIGURE 5.12 Page layout programs like QuarkXPress allow you to create some striking special effects without leaving the program.

TIP

How to try before you buy? Be sure to thoroughly evaluate any alternatives you may be considering. Ask the software's publisher for a demonstration version of the product. Many publishers produce save-disabled and print-disabled versions (that don't allow you to save or print the files these products create) for evaluation purposes. Another source for evaluating a specific product is through your local product representative or consultant. Most software publishers can tell you what stores in your area are approved or who is a qualified consultant or specialist for their software products. Such people are often exceptional sources of real-world information about products.

Drawing Programs

Just as PageMaker and QuarkXPress will always be competing for lead-dog position in the page-composition market, there will always be fierce competition among the major PostScript drawing program publishers for first place. The feature wars in this product area are just as prevalent as in the page-layout market, creating ever more complex, diverse, and capable software products.

Who needs a PostScript drawing program? Well, not everyone, but almost everyone can benefit from the advantages of PostScript object-oriented drawing. The benefits of PostScript art include compatibility between applications and platforms; scalable, resolution-independent, object-based art; precision; and versatility.

Here are some of the results you can expect from a PostScript drawing program (see Figures 5.13and 5.14).

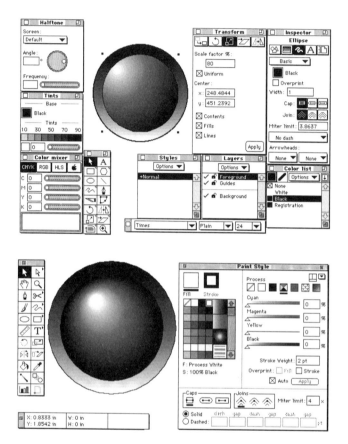

FIGURES 5.13 and 5.14 Remember that you can easily import these images into your page-layout applications. You can resize and retain the fine resolution of your imagesetter at any size and create accurate and precise separations automatically.

PostScript drawing programs work by creating objects defined in terms of *paths* and *fills*. Paths are the outlines that define the shape of an object, and fills are the contents of the objects. Paths can be assigned specific colors, tints, weights, and end caps (see Figures 5.15 and 5.16). Any area outlined by a path can be filled with any color or shade of color, or even no fill, creating a transparent object (see Figure 5.17).

FIGURE 5.15 A Beziér curve path with handles.

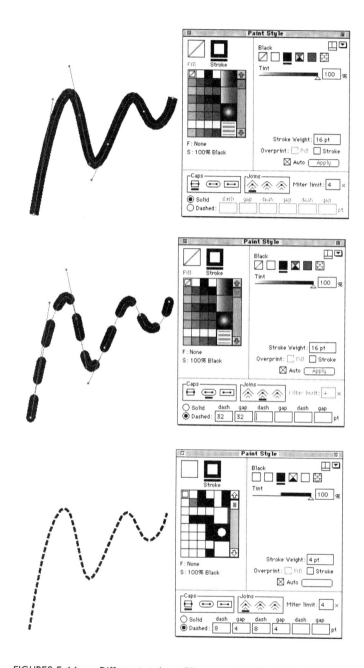

FIGURES 5.16a-c Different styles of lines created in Adobe Illustrator.

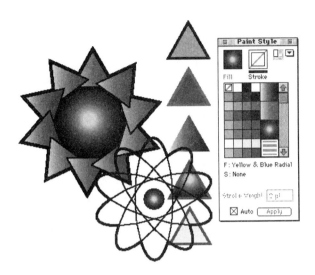

FIGURE 5.17 Shapes are easy to manipulate.

Even fonts can be defined shapes with fills and paths determined by the user (see Figure 5.18).

FIGURE 5.18 One of the great benefits of object-oriented drawing programs is the ability to quickly create exact duplicates of shapes. For example, it's easy to create a simple drop shadow by duplicating a shape and recoloring with a shade of black.

FreeHand Versus Illustrator

The two big contenders in the PostScript drawing market are FreeHand and Illustrator. Both are exceptional tools for creating precise artwork, and the two companies have been involved in a protracted feature war since the competition for this market began.

Both FreeHand and Illustrator offer precise control and versatility for creating PostScript art. Both use a comprehensive system of floating palettes for controlling and defining objects. While the advantages of one over the other can only be obtained through user experience, a few of the differences are listed here:

※ FreeHand and Illustrator use similar tools for creating objects in the respective program. FreeHand offers enhanced automation in handling and defining objects created in the program using an Inspector palette, which offers a simple point-and-click interface for defining objects (see Figure 5.19).

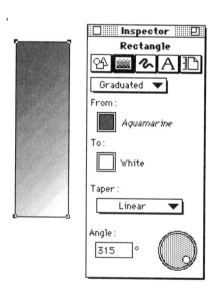

FIGURE 5.19 The Freehand Inspector palette.

❋   Illustrator offers a system of palettes for controlling and defining objects with the same fine precision as FreeHand. In addition, Illustrator offers a unique chart and graph drawing utility built into the program (see Figure 5.20).

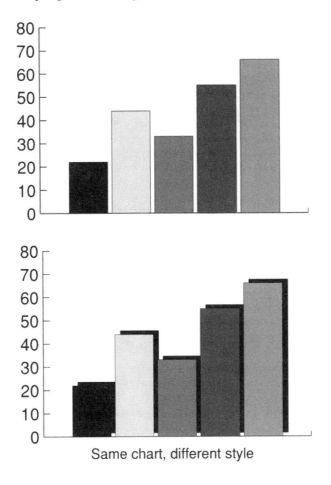

Same chart, different style

FIGURE 5.20 The chart capabilities of Freehand.

❋   With all the benefits of PostScript artwork, Illustrator's charts and graphs are also changeable and customizable "on the fly" (see Figure 5.21).

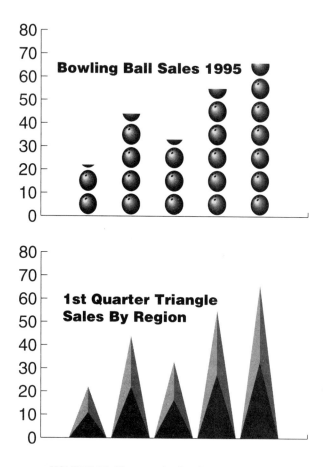

FIGURE 5.21 Illustrator's charting capabilities.

A PostScript drawing program offers the artist precision, creativity, and versatility not found in other software products. It's worth your consideration as an essential software tool.

Non-PostScript (or QuickDraw) Drawing Programs

There are a few non-PostScript drawing programs on the market today that rely on Apple's QuickDraw imaging model to create and print objects.

Using similar tools and interfaces as PostScript drawing programs, these products can create impressive works without using PostScript. Products such as MacDraw Pro, Claris Impact, and Canvas make great art-creation tools but receive mixed reviews when it comes to creating production art (see Figure 5.22). Check with your local user's group and imaging service bureau for actual real-world experiential advice on each product's relative worth to you.

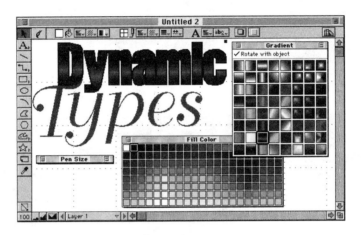

FIGURE 5.22 The palette from Claris Draw.

Image Manipulation

With the beginning of this digital revolution, new art forms and capabilities have been made possible with tools like Adobe Photoshop, Fractal Painter, and Aldus PhotoStyler. Products like these present the artist with incredible tools for manipulating scanned images and creating remarkable "painted" images. They work by manipulating or processing images at the pixel level to create their special visual effects.

With products like these, the designer or illustrator can manipulate scanned images for better reproduction and output, adjusting color levels, gray component, and undercolor removal—tasks that previously required extremely complex and expensive hardware and specially skilled operators (see Figure 5.23).

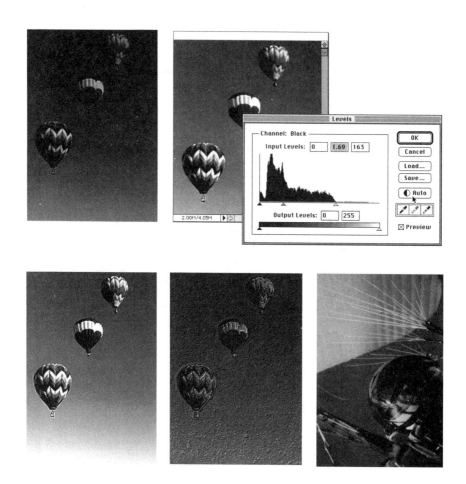

FIGURES 5.23a-e Correction tasks easily made by computer.

They also offer an impressive array of automated artistic enhancements and effects in the form of filters that work with the programs (see Figure 5.24). You can create remarkable textures and visual effects quickly and easily for your own illustrative works of art.

FIGURE 5.24 Digital art.

You will undoubtedly be called upon at one time or another to retouch or manipulate a scanned image or perhaps to improve the halftone output or create a completely artistic representation. Image manipulation and digital painting tools will be absolutely indispensable to you for these tasks.

Image Translation

In addition to manipulating images, products like Adobe Photoshop serve as effective image-translation tools. For example, in Photoshop you can easily open a common **JPEG PICT** file that you've copied from a standard QuickTime digital-video animation and convert it to a grayscale TIFF image. Simply choose **Grayscale** under the Mode menu (see Figure 5.25). Then choose **Save as...** from the File menu and choose **TIFF** from the File Format pop-up menu (see Figure 5.26).

FIGURE 5.25 The greyscale selection in Photoshop.

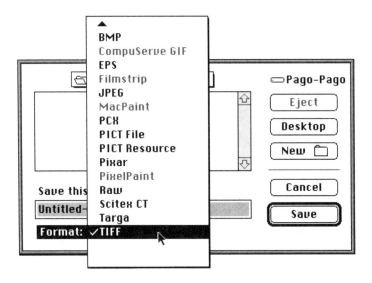

FIGURE 5.26 Saving the image.

Easily and quickly, this capability will help you create TIFF images that can be easily controlled for fine halftone output in your page-layout program. If your system doesn't include Photoshop or a comparable image-manipulation program, there is another method you can use for translating images between formats. There are plenty of freeware and shareware image-viewing utilities available through online services. These also perform the functions of converting images from one format to another.

Fonts

Where do all these wild fonts come from? Does everyone you know seem to have twice as many fonts as you? Don't you wish you had a magic font source to provide fonts on demand?

There are plenty of font vendors in the market today, offering an incredible variety of fonts fitting thousands of looks and design concepts. You can purchase huge volumes of fonts for $50 or so, delivered on CD-ROM or on handfuls of disks.

 While attractive and decorative, some fonts don't always print well. To test whether or not these fonts are efficiently designed and prone to clean printing, create some sample text in your favorite PostScript drawing program and convert the text to outlines (see Figure 5.27).

FIGURE 5.27 Fonts converted to outlines.

Look closely at the outlined fonts. Look for uneven joints between paths on a simple curve (see Figure 5.28).

FIGURE 5.28 An uneven curve.

Another potential problem area is the number of control points. If the text seems to have an inordinate amount of control points (see Figure 5.29), there is a greater-than-average chance that your imagesetter will have problems imaging a page full of this text.

FIGURE 5.29 Control points on the outline.

Another source of fonts that you might want to consider are the various online services such as CompuServe and America Online. Members may post their own font creations to the various publishing and art forums (see Figure 5.30).

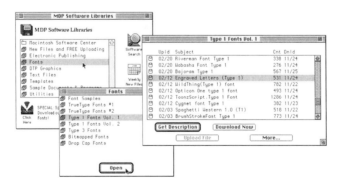

FIGURE 5.30 The America Online font forum.

If you get fonts from such sources, be especially conscious of copyright laws and respect the intellectual property of the creators. If there's a shareware fee solicited, it's probably much less expensive than that of commercially distributed fonts.

NOTE

Contacting the actual creators of fonts and other shareware products is easier than ever. Most products posted to online forums will have a contact source via email or telephone. If you find a font that strikes your fancy in one of the online forums, don't be shy about contacting the creator to compliment his or her work. It's easy, it's good karma, and it makes a great impression.

Font-Management Utilities

Collecting fonts can turn into an arcane hobby, like collecting record albums. It's easy to get started, and before you know it, you've amassed a sizable volume of fonts without much effort. With so many fonts in your system, you'll need some way to organize and maintain fonts in a simple and efficient manner. Font-management utilities allow you to classify and sort your font collections by types, by client, or by project, all without occupying precious system memory. You can also define groups of font families that can be activated with a few keystrokes. Add a font-management utility to your workstation wish list.

Summary

A well-rounded and functional collection of software with a comprehensive group of capabilities will include:

※ A page-layout or composition software such as QuarkXPress or Aldus PageMaker.

※ A PostScript drawing program such as Adobe Illustrator or Aldus Freehand.

※ Image-manipulation software such as Adobe Photoshop, Aldus PhotoStyler, or Fractal Design Painter

* A collection of Type 1 PostScript fonts.
* A font-management utility such as Suitcase.

What These Programs Do

Page-layout software offers the ability to compose pages, including graphics and type, with precise control over both.

PostScript drawing software provides capabilities for creating object-based artwork such as technical renderings, special type treatments, and diagrams with extreme precision and versatility.

Image-manipulation software allows you to manipulate and convert pixel-based scanned or painted images using special effects that used to be found only at outside services.

Fonts and font-management utilities allow you to offer a wider variety of special typefaces and type treatments when used in concert with your other page-layout and drawing programs.

Does It All Work as Advertised?

Getting the straight information on whether a particular brand or product performs as advertised is a fairly simple task if you own a telephone. Some easy-to-reach and objective sources are specialists and consultants, users groups, and your neighborhood service bureaus. These people work with these products day in and day out. Don't be shy about asking them for a real-world assessment of each product's relative worth, capabilities, and compatibilities.

The biggest issue after features and capabilities is printability. All the bells and whistles in the world will do you no good if the documents you create will not print. Get your service bureau's advice and ask about their experience with the following:

* TrueType versus Adobe Type 1
* FreeHand versus Illustrator
* PageMaker versus QuarkXPress

148

Remember: your business, your reputation, and your mortgage payment all directly or indirectly rely on the ability of your system to perform as advertised. Projects that take longer to print (or don't print at all) and projects that print incorrectly will cost you money. Whatever steps you can take now to make sure everything works well together will pay off in the long run.

Concept: Your Dream System

If you could have everything you desired in a computer system—speed, capacity, capability with no limits—what would that look like?

The ultimate studio would have to have a wall-sized video display, unlimited screen real estate, room for an unlimited number of windows to open simultaneously, and all the tool palettes in the known universe floating in their own space—all within arm's reach. For that matter, it would also have to be in three dimensions, displaying a virtual operating system that interacts with you by voice, eye movement, and physical motion.

The operating system would have to interact with you in an intuitive and invisible fashion, using all three dimensions and all five senses to operate. It would sense your intentions and assume a simple intelligence and personality of its own, complementary to yours.

To work with text, you would simply look at the holographic image of writing tools and paper and say, "Let's write a letter, Hal." The operating system would automatically launch the appropriate utilities (which would of course be waiting in an instantaneous RAM partition with all the other launchable applications in your system). Similarly, you might work with an image-editing or painting program by telling your computer which tool to use and looking directly at the area of the image on which you wanted to work. Perhaps you'll move your hand through the virtual three-dimensional space that a holographic image of the tool would occupy floating in the air around your hand.

The operating system would answer your telephone calls for you, schedule your appointments, and remind you of all your scheduled tasks. It would interact with you as an intelligent agent that could take the form of anything you can imagine, even a ferret wearing a bow tie and dinner jacket.

Your computer would have an unlimited instantaneous memory capacity with all your applications running concurrently so you could instantly launch, cut, and paste between applications. Your system would understand natural language, taking dictation and instructions by voice commands, eye movements, or physical motion, sensing all of these through an innocuous lens and sensory system that would reside somewhere in the room with you as you work.

Your printer would produce holographic, photographically real imaging with animated and sound-capable documents. It might exist as a room unto itself off of your working area or office and could be shared by anyone else in your work group. It would print automatically and instantly (no wait-ing), composing parts of the document as you create it, keeping the evolving document in its own virtual RAM partition. By the time you said, "Print this," the document would be nearly completely imaged and waiting for you by the time you reached into your output tray in your desk drawer.

There wouldn't be any more unwieldy wires or cables for networking capabilities. Networking and communication services would take place using the atmosphere itself or the Earth's magnetic field as the transmission medium. Your workstation might have a simple antenna or lens as a trans-ceiver and would be able to communicate with any other device on the planet. Imagine being able to communicate with any earth inhabitant (or their intelligent agent who might appear in any imaginable form) via an instant holographic link.

Finally, your work would be transmitted directly to your clients electronically, and it would be output on their imaging device as it was being completed, so that you would have creative direction as you work. Changes would be instant and painless, as the client made suggestions to your intelligent agent, who would relay them to you via a small window that appears in your work area on-screen and would even help you by making its own suggestions or actions on-screen as you work.

You see that the paradigm for success in your field has moved from the ownership of hardware to expression of ideas. The key to success belongs not to the person who owns the biggest fastest machines, but to the one with the best ideas and creativity. These tools of the future are what empower us with such capability.

Chapter 6

Choosing Your Service Bureau

Where to Get Your Work Produced

It was a lot easier to choose a service bureau when there was only one in town and all they provided was single-color output on RC paper. Today, things are different; there is a wide selection of services, products, and capabilities among which to choose. Most service bureaus today offer a wide range of services from simple one-color output to high-resolution color proofs and separations. This chapter will help you make an informed choice when selecting a service provider and will give you a checklist for determining which service source is right for you.

In-House Versus Service Bureau

As this industry has matured, there has been a shift in the amount and types of services offered by printers, typesetters, and specialty production houses in graphics and printing production. It has been projected that to stay competitive, a printing house must now offer digital prepress production services, just as small typesetter and prepress production houses are now being forced to offer printing services.

This has obviously led to a segmenting of the industry. Smaller service providers are forced to move from having limited specialization to offering a larger menu of services such as offset printing and enhanced digital services to stay competitive. Larger printers are having to invest in new technology to avoid seeing more of their preparatory-services income taken by the smaller service bureaus. Naturally, this has led to varying results as businesses scramble to hire qualified and skilled operators for the new equipment while striving to provide the best services possible to their clients and encouraging growth in the business.

In many ways, it makes sense to keep your prepress services in the same building as your printing services. The line of responsibility remains shorter and is more easily traced in the event of a problem. Time and expense for proofs and deliveries are reduced, and the same people who are applying the ink to the paper are there to help you make decisions on dot gain and color balance. When you arrive for your press inspection, the very people who created the final output are close at hand for advice and assistance.

On the other hand, if your project is being printed across the country (or in another country), then having your prepress services close to home keeps your control within easy reach. You can create your work, print your proofs, run your negatives, print more proofs, and be certain that everything you do is under control before sending your negatives off to the printer. If the printer you've chosen does not have digital capabilities in-house, then taking care of the prepress chores at your local service bureau helps you keep production expenses down and gives you more control over quality in-house.

Choosing Your Service Bureau

Following is a comprehensive overview of what to look for when choosing your service bureau. Ask yourself—and them—these questions so that you'll be able to make an informed decision.

Capabilities

1. What are the primary services and capabilities offered by this business?
2. What is the maximum output resolution of the company's equipment? It may not be a standard, and not all imagesetters are created equal.

3. Do they offer color proofs? What kinds of color printers do they use? What are the costs?

4. How long have they been in this business? How experienced are their equipment operators? What's their background? Are they primarily graphic artists or computer operators?

5. Are there any types of removable storage media that they *do not* accept? If you are saving your large files onto 5.25-inch magneto-optical disks for transport to the service bureau, and they don't have a 5.25-inch magneto-optical drive to read those disks, you might want to look elsewhere for your output service provider.

Services

1. Does the company offer assistance in proofing your work? What kinds of proofs can it produce? Can the company make high-resolution four-color proofs like Chromalins, color keys, or match-prints in-house? Are the company's employees skilled enough to recognize potential production problems in the proofing stage?

2. Does the company stand behind its work? What is its customer service policy? How does it handle conflict-resolution and quality-assurance concerns?

3. Does the company offer delivery services? Does it have a turnaround time guarantee?

4. Everyone has a fax machine; does the company support a 24-hour electronic bulletin board service? At what speeds can you connect to its service? Is the work order process automated? Will the company supply the telecommunications software to you at no charge?

In addition to capability and service questions, there are a few questions you might ask that will provide insight into the character of the business. With what kind of people are you hoping to do business? You might ask:

1. What is the company's daily volume of work? How many workstations and imagesetters are used there? Will the employees have time to pay individual attention to your job if there's ever a problem?

2. How often does the company change or refresh its processor's chemistry? Is the output room environmentally controlled? In some cases, small variations in temperature, humidity, and the freshness of the chemistry can create changes in the character and density of your halftone dots.

If your project requires changes to one plate of a page with four-color separations, make sure that you rerun all four negatives for production. Subtle changes in the halftone output on one plate caused by any of the reasons mentioned here could change the color balance or halftone moiré.

Consider that your service bureau is a silent partner with some significant influence on your business success. It makes sense that you should get to know your partner as closely as possible. It's worth your time to schedule a visit or two to your candidate service bureaus and see for yourself the kind of business that you are asking to support you.

Here are some things to look for during your visit to potential service bureaus:

1. Is the shop clean? Is the equipment well cared for? Is your project going to be well cared for?

2. Do the employees look happy? Are they attentive to their work and their clients?

3. How old is the equipment? Is the company using equipment that is up-to-date? Is it using the current system software and current versions of your software? Is the company likely to encounter compatibility problems with your files?

While you're there, you might want to ask a few additional questions:

1. Is the company willing to give you the names of some of their other clients as references? If it is, make sure you call these references and ask direct questions about service and quality.

2. Is the company proud of its work? Does it have a portfolio of samples?

3. Does the company offer other services? Is it competent to intervene in files with obvious (or even subtle) production problems?

4. Will the company take you to lunch? (Will they buy?) Getting to know your sales or service representative on a first-name basis can never hurt; and hearing them tell anecdotal tales of their best and worst jobs will give you some personal insight into how they solve tough client problems.

5. Does the company work overnight? Will anyone be there if you need a late-night emergency reprint while your printer is holding the presses?

6. Does the company offer rush services, and at what price premium? You may initially choke on a 400% premium for a two-hour turn-around, until you need something in one hour.

When interviewing prospective service bureau candidates, you might want to try keeping track of each contact with a simple form listing their vital statistics, services offered and general impressions (see Figure 6.1).

Here's a summary of the questions you might ask:

* Name of business
* Contact name
* Address
* Title
* City
* Telephone (voice)
* Telephone (fax)
* Bulletin board system number
* Capabilities
* Highest resolution possible
* Best reliable halftone screen
* Film and paper output available
* Largest page size available
* Software products used
* Types of removable media accepted

* Color output services available
* Services
* Delivery service available
* Proofing assistance available
* Experience level
* Qualified in major software products
* Operator's experience level
* Experienced in graphics production
* Customer-service representative assigned to my account
* General business questions
* Billing practices
* Volume of business daily
* Percentage color/separations
* Time between chemistry changes
* Environmentally controlled processing room
* How long in this business
* Customer references provided? (3)
* Other services offered
* Lunch
* Portfolio

FIGURE 6.1 List of questions to ask your service bureau.

What Makes a Good Client?

How can you be sure that your service bureau will love you and look forward to the files you bring to them? (The answer to this question is not volume.) *Communication.* Your service bureau will be your friend if you spend time during each and every job discussing your objectives and output needs.

Knowing exactly what you're after helps your service bureau make better decisions about how best to proceed with your work. The service bureau's employees will know the results you need and expect—and most importantly, they'll be able to make suggestions about how to get those results quickly and efficiently.

You can be a good client by knowing what you know—and don't know—about the computer, software, and prepress production process, and by sharing what you know and don't know with your service bureau. Then, knowing what your capabilities and knowledge level are, the service bureau can help guide you through the process with suggestions and help at every step.

When you're investigating service bureaus and asking the questions on your Service Bureau Qualification Survey form, be sure to ask them what they're looking for in a client. By making this small gesture of cooperation, you'll surely endear yourself to them as someone who is serious about a successful collaborative relationship.

It's a Perfect World

Good news, it's a perfect world. Your worries are over! There are three levels of service in a perfect world:

* The user knows everything and doesn't ever need any help or advice.

* The user doesn't know anything. The service bureau knows everything and offers their advice and time for free.

* Both user and service bureau know enough to get each other into trouble, but share their experiences and knowledge in a sympathetic and constructive manner, thereby providing great value for the price and offering exceptional savings and service.

In the first example, the user (that's you) already knows everything there is to know about the inner workings of the software, the files, the computer, the design, and the production and printing process. The user also knows everything about the high-resolution output device onto which his project is going to be imaged. In fact, the service bureau operator is so confident of this fact that he needs only to press the **Print** button once for each job that comes through the door. It's a perfect world. Everyone sleeps comfortably each night without worry or concern. The jobs are delivered on time, invoices are paid promptly, and everyone makes money.

The second perfect-world example proposes that the user (that's you), while knowledgeable and of above-average intelligence, doesn't have to know anything. The imaging service bureau knows everything there is to know about the inner workings of the software, the files, and the computer as well as the design, production, and printing process. The service bureau also knows everything about the high-resolution output device onto which the project is going to be imaged, consults with the client, and offers advice and time for free in a demonstration of good business cooperation. In this world, the user can create any sort of digital file, with many third-party TrueType and Type 1 fonts, EPS halftones, and complex PostScript images defying all conventional wisdom and common sense, and the service bureau (your friends) will have no trouble at all imaging the files, making all necessary corrections at no charge to you.

Finally, our third perfect-world example has both user and service bureau knowing just enough about the inner workings of the software, files, computer, design, production, printing, and high-resolution output device onto which the project is going to be imaged to get each other into trouble. Recognizing this fact, the two sides share their experiences and knowledge in a sympathetic and constructive manner, thereby providing great value for the price and offering exceptional savings and service to the user (you). In this world, the user and the service bureau (your friends) discuss in detail the objectives you hope to achieve with this project, the requirements to achieve those objectives, and all potential problems that might occur.

You might begin by showing them a color comp or sketch of the finished project as you envision it and then discussing strategies for creating the file needed to accomplish the design. A good service bureau will be able to make credible suggestions about the best ways to achieve the effects you're after and avoid production errors that will cost you time and money. Talk about the size and type of output you'll require (this could be as simple as RC paper output in one color or as complex as wrong-reading, emulsion-side-up negatives), the time required to image the job, the deadlines and completion schedule, and projected costs involved. You may want to obtain a written estimate just to get everything on paper. Add a copy of the estimate to your job file for later reference.

The Real World

Although it is a perfect world, because the physics of entropy seem to be concentrated around the computer industry, the work we produce in it isn't always as perfect as we'd like it to be. Sometimes unexpected results and undocumented features in the software, hardware, or even in the process itself can cause a few delays in our workflow. An important technique to remember when confronted with these surprises is not to lose our heads.

The universe is in constant motion. Equipment, printers, RIPs, and human beings can only work so fast (assuming the speed of light is an absolute constant), but the brick wall of a deadline seems to be relatively steadfast throughout the process. Acceptance of these facts and focusing on solutions instead of consequences can help you cut down on the volume of ulcer medication you consume.

A good service bureau is as involved and interested in your success as you are. The laws of natural selection and evolution eventually remove from the food chain the ones that aren't. Count on the support and assistance of your service bureau or skilled computer graphics consultant to get you through the challenging times.

In the real world, service bureaus have probably dealt with most commonly encountered production problems long before you walked in with yours. If they haven't, most have access to higher-end technical support from the software publishers themselves and can get to the bottom of most problems in short order. Most production problems are easily solved with a little prevention and awareness, not to mention experience.

The most common problem a service bureau will encounter when imaging a file for you is missing high-resolution images in a page-layout document. It's an easy step to overlook when shipping your files for imaging, in spite of built-in features in software like QuarkXPress to help you avoid the problem. Following is a simple way to proof your work completely before incurring expensive faulty output charges.

Of course, you've been printing laser proofs of your work as you've been completing each stage of your production, and it's looked great every step of the way. So it's always a surprise when the service bureau calls and says your file is missing a high-resolution image. The best way to get a reliable proof of the final file you're going to send to your service bureau is to follow these four simple steps:

1. If you're using QuarkXPress, choose **Collect for Output** under your File menu and choose a new folder on your desktop as a destination. (If you're not using QuarkXPress, copy your document and all associated image files to a folder on your desktop.)

2. Copy this folder to the removable cartridge you're going to use to transport the file to the service bureau.

3. Move the entire original folder containing your document and all associated image files from your internal hard disk to another removable cartridge for permanent archival storage. You may want to compress the original folder and its contents using a compression utility for more efficient use of storage space.

4. Finally, open the document again from the removable cartridge that you'll use to transport the files to the service bureau, and print another proof, both composite and separations if applicable. Since you've removed the original file and images, the only data available to the program will be on the removable cartridge. If you missed, lost, renamed, or modified any of the linked image files, you'll find out when you do this and can go looking for them so that you can include them in the file you send to your service bureau.

This way you're sure to include all the files and images necessary for flawless output. This simple process will make your life much easier and increase your peace of mind. Your service bureau will thank you for making their life easier too. And best of all, your friends and family will thank you for being in a better mood when you see them after regular business hours.

Concept: The Perfect Service Bureau

Look around. You may have a perfect service bureau right in your own home town. The perfect service bureau:

* Is close to home. Even though you may prefer to send your files via modem, it's convenient to stop in for a visit now and then or to help troubleshoot problem files.

* Is staffed and managed by people who are competent with computers and have a strong background in graphic production. On staff are "domain experts" who specialize in the software products you use and who know their way around a printing press and production facility.

* Will assign a representative to handle your account. This person's responsibilities include knowing your system and being familiar with the kinds of projects you submit for output. This person will also have knowledge of the printing process and will be courteous and helpful with advice to help you create flawless production art every time.

* Encourages communication with you. They will take pains to make sure all the details are covered as your job is entered into their system.

* Will have a computer workstation available for your use, should you require any last-minute adjustments when you drop off your files. Maybe this workstation is placed in a quiet office, apart from the regular hustle and bustle of business.

* Also has a complete printing and high-resolution proofing service available, so you can have your projects printed right on the premises after proofing your output.

* Will offer delivery services at no additional charge (with a sufficient page volume of work).

Do you live near the perfect service bureau? Their locations and telephone numbers are a closely guarded secret in the industry. Naturally, in a world rife with mediocrity, these "super" bureaus are protective of their identities and location, lest they be over-run with business. Look around and find one, but don't tell anyone.

Chapter 7

Getting Your Work Ready to Print

* Items to be most aware of and their importance in getting the output the reader expects
* What the service bureau needs, and why
* The value of a good proof, types of proofs
* Preparing your job for service bureau output: the complete step-by-step checklist

Getting Ready

Now then, you've put your best creative work onto electronic pages, applied countless layers of Photoshop filters, tweaked every character of type in the layout down to the finest detail... Now what? How do you take your work from what appears on your computer screen to what gets printed on paper? How do you know that what you see is what you get... or what you want?

This chapter describes every step of the process and will help you get the best camera-ready output possible. Following the simple checklist in this chapter and spending a few minutes talking with your friendly service bureau will invariably save you a few dollars and a ton of headaches.

It might help you to create a simple checklist based on your service bureau's work-order form to make sure that you're sending everything the service bureau needs to image the document correctly.

The very first step in getting high-resolution output from your service bureau is determining exactly what type of output you need. We'll discuss the requirements for each major type of output from one-color on paper to four-color separated film, and we will go over all the services required for each.

Single-Color Jobs

One-color jobs are among the simplest to produce because they do not require as much intervention from either the production artist or the press operator as using two or more colors does. There are no complex registration issues to confront, proofs are easier and less expensive to obtain, and changes are easier to accomplish.

What You Need to Know for the Best Results

What is the medium? Coated or uncoated paper? Newspaper or magazine? Uncoated papers are more absorbent, creating a potential for ink spread. Printing on common newsprint requires a coarser halftone screen output to prevent ink spread and clogged halftones. Coated papers tend not to absorb as much ink, allowing for tighter halftone screens.

Ask your printer for advice on halftone line screen frequency. How tight should you specify your halftones? How many lines per inch? Knowing this can help you decide at what resolution you will scan your grayscale images. Your service bureau knows its materials, supplies, and environment very well, and it can give you credible advice on what specifications to give your images for the best halftone output possible.

For images, you'll also want to ask about photographic halftone range. At what point does the given printing process fail to reproduce a small black or white dot? What's the smallest halftone dot that can be reproduced at a preferred halftone line frequency? You may want to consider adjusting this information in your grayscale images using an image editing software program like Adobe Photoshop.

Technique: Optimizing Your Scanned Data for a Full Grayscale Range

To get the best halftone images, you need to understand that each printer, printing process, and paper and ink combination has an optimum value for indicating white and black on a page to create a full range of grays. Ask your service bureau what their white and black halftone dot values are and then adjust the grayscale output accordingly using a product like Adobe Photoshop. Follow these steps:

1. Your service bureau might tell you that they can hold a 10% dot for an absolute white and 90% of solid black in an image, given the paper, inks, and printing process it is using. You can optimize your grayscale/halftone image to take advantage of these capabilities and get the absolute best halftone output. (See Figures 7.1 and 7.2.)

FIGURE 7.1 This area is not actually white. Rather, it is the threshold where a 1% halftone dot loses definition.

FIGURE 7.2 This area is not solid black. It is actually about 99% of black, the threshold where the printing process can no longer hold a small enough white dot. It is essentially a solid black dot, but the data defines it as being 99% of solid.

2. Open your grayscale image in Photoshop and choose **Show Info** under the Windows menu to display the Information palette (see Figure 7.3).Notice that as you move the cursor around your image, the value for K (or black) is shown as a percentage.

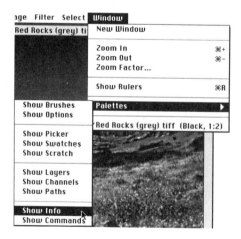

FIGURE 7.3 The Show Info Window.

3. Now choose the Image menu, then choose **Levels** from the pop-up menu that appears (see Figure 7.4).

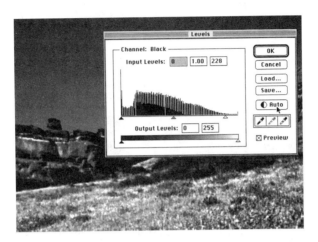

FIGURE 7.4 The Levels dialog.

The Levels dialog shows a histogram of the distribution of gray levels present in your document. This may be unevenly dispersed (for any number of reasons, including quality of the scanned image data or the type of image itself). You can drag the white, black, or midpoint triangles to make very coarse adjustments. (See how the image changes as you slide these triangles around.)

To make the most accurate adjustment, choose the white eyedropper tool and move it around over a white part of the image until the K value in the Info palette matches the white percentage that your service bureau suggested (see Figure 7.5). Then click the mouse in that position to tell Photoshop that for this image, this point is the lightest value that should be present. You'll see the entire image adjust from this value.

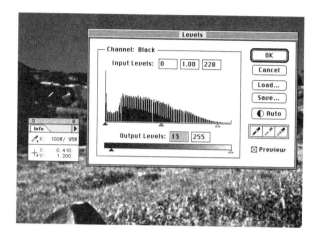

FIGURE 7.5 Using the Levels Info palette.

4. Now choose the black eyedropper and move it around in your image until the K value in the Info palette shows the same value as your service bureau suggested for a solid black.

Compare this image to the image as it was when we started this process. You'll notice a very subtle change in the appearance, but one that will give you the best halftone output possible (see Figure 7.6).

FIGURE 7.6 Better halftone output.

Next, you'll need to consult with your service bureau to determine whether they prefer your camera-ready output to be on RC (resin-coated) paper or on film, and then whether they need positives; negatives; right-reading, emulsion-down; or other output types.

Does your service bureau own the appropriate fonts to image your job? Most service bureaus have extensive licensed font collections, but it never hurts to ask. Make sure that their fonts are identical to yours in type and publisher. A TrueType font named Times will not image the way Adobe's Type 1 Times font will. If you set your type using TrueType and the service bureau uses the Type 1 equivalent, your text will certainly re-flow and, in some situations, cause the imagesetter to crash.

Finally, make sure that when you transport your file by whatever medium you are using (disk, cartridge, tape, modem), you include all the relevant images with your document. This includes PostScript drawings as well as scanned images. The **Collect for Output** command under the QuarkXPress File menu is a wonderful time- and headache-saver for making sure you have all the correct images included with your job (as well as a summary of all your fonts, production notes, etc.).

Call ahead to confirm your service bureau's production schedule. Can they meet your deadline without any rush charges? Will they be able to provide a little consulting time to help you proof your work? Can they deliver the final product back to you?

Two or More Printed Colors

When printing two or more spot colors, you're adding a marginal level of difficulty over printing a single color to paper. All the previous concerns regarding paper, ink, and halftone values still apply. The additional complexity you're adding to the project is in registration and trapping. You must make sure that all colors appear where they are supposed to.

You can add one more question to ask your service bureau: To what precision can it register (match up the locations of) adjoining colors? Some jobs requiring fine precision, to perhaps half a dot, may be problematic in some situations.

Traps, Chokes, and Spreads

As described previously, shifting or stretching paper, misaligned machinery, and even minor production errors can cause improperly printed registration of some adjoining colors. Luckily, your page-layout software allows you to adjust the trapping values to help compensate for these problems.

For smaller two- and three-color jobs using simple spot colors, the costs for engaging additional RIP services such as TrapWise and/or Dolev to create automatic traps may not be justified. If your project is relatively simple, the automatic trapping feature in your page-layout software may be enough to handle the job itself.

A good rule of thumb for defining and controlling traps in multicolor printing jobs is: If your project does not involve any imported EPS drawing artwork, then the automatic trapping function in your page-layout software is probably capable of handling the job without your intervention. If your project contains imported EPS graphics from a PostScript drawing program, then the traps must be established in the program that created them.

TIP

The one big point to remember about manually trapping PostScript objects in a drawing program is that the traps you create are all relatively scaled with the image. This means that if you establish a 0.1-point trap on an object in Illustrator and then import the EPS graphic to your page-layout software and reduce the size of the image by 50%, your resulting trap will be only 0.05 point. Be aware of this when creating your PostScript artwork, and ask your printer for a trapping value recommendation.

Technique: Creating a Simple Trap in Adobe Illustrator

Here's a quick way to create a trap of a PostScript object in Adobe Illustrator or Aldus FreeHand. This works very well for less complex artwork.

Create a solid object in your drawing program (see Figure 7.7). Specify one of the solid colors that will be present in your final page-layout document.

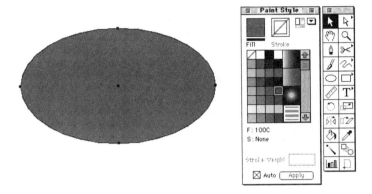

FIGURE 7.7 An object.

Create another object or type outline (see Figure 7.8) and define it as being filled solidly with another color that will be present in your page-layout document.

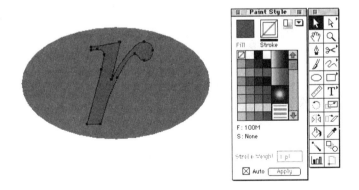

FIGURE 7.8 Another object.

If left to the program's defaults, the topmost object would knock out of the background object with no trap (see Figure 7.9).

FIGURE 7.9 Layered images.

To create an overlapping trap area, select the object and apply a stroke of the same color as the interior of the object. Here's the big tip: Make sure that the stroke is designated to overprint (see Figures 7.10 and 7.11).

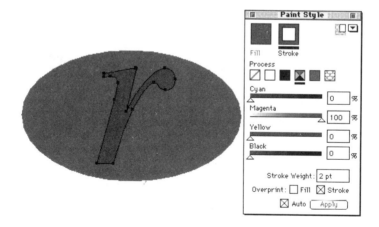

FIGURE 7.10 Stroked overpoint.

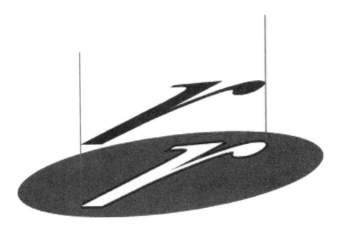

FIGURE 7.11 An interior stroke.

Remember that the stroke surrounding your object is measured from the center of the path. If you've defined a width of two points, then the actual overlapping area is only the outside half of the stroke, one point (see Figure 7.12). Set your stroke width to twice your expected trap value.

FIGURE 7.12 A 1 point stroke.

Special Cases

If you're importing EPS graphics created with a PostScript drawing program and you are using a custom color created for this document, you need to make sure that the exact same color (with the exact same name) exists in the page-layout program in order for you to create proper separations. For example, if you've created a spot color named **Fred** in your PostScript illustration, you need to make sure there's a color named **Fred** in your page-layout program in order for the art to separate properly. Both major page-layout programs have incorporated this as an automatic feature in the current revs

If you're creating duotones in an image-editing program (like Photoshop), there's a simple but necessary step you need to perform in order for the duotones to separate properly in your page-layout program. Compose your duotone image using two Pantone colors as defined in the program's color palette (see Figure 7.13).

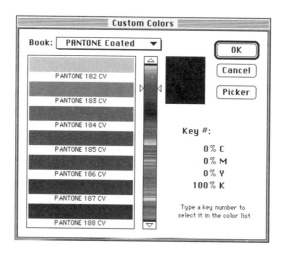

FIGURE 7.13 Select the color.

When you've finished composing your image, save it as a **Continuous Tone EPS Document** using the pop-up menu in the Save dialog box (see Figure 7.14).

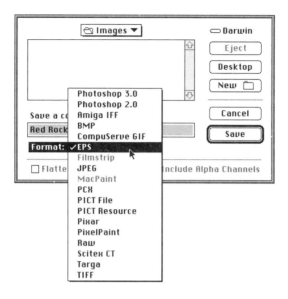

FIGURE 7.14 Save the image as EPS.

Import the image as you ordinarily would to your page-layout document. Make sure that you've added both Pantone colors to your color palette to assure correct separation. If you want a picture border to trap the image (if it's a standard-shaped image), you can define a border within the page-layout program and designate it to overprint (see Figure 7.15).

FIGURE 7.15 A duotone.

175

Registration

You can help your service bureau create a better product faster and more easily (and without additional preparation charges) by printing your document with trim lines and registration marks. You could create these manually, but both major page-layout products provide this feature as an option in the Print dialog box.

Registration marks on the negatives help the printer align all the plates to produce correct registration in the final product (see Figure 7.16). Registration marks appear on all plates in exactly the same position, allowing the printer to see if any plates are misaligned.

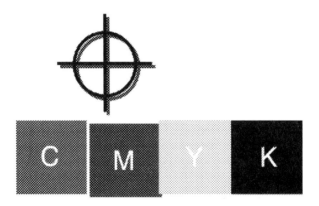

FIGURE 7.16 The magenta plate is slightly out of alignment, or mis-registered.

Four or More Colors

As you move into more sophisticated production, beyond two- and three-color work, your biggest concerns will be in making sure that your process colors precisely match your reference material. Whether you're matching a PMS color swatch or a full-color photograph, color-matching software and monitor calibration can only go so far in that endeavor. For that matter, color proofs are not always accurate to the final product. Color matching is often a hit-or-miss prospect that can't always be guaranteed before your project is on the press. Your best insurance is to schedule a press inspection of your project while it is being produced.

While products like ColorSync and EFIColor go a long way toward creating a more matchable color image across several devices, there is a still a long way to go in getting a reliable color proof. A basic and inexpensive color proof can be had from even the lowest color-inkjet printer. This will at least give you some idea of where your colors lie relative to each other, even if the colors are not absolutely accurate. The color proof that will most closely resemble your final printed product will be a chromalin or MatchPrint, made from the negatives generated for your project. Unfortunately, these are also the most expensive color proofs to make. It's a good strategy to let the chromalin or MatchPrint proof be the last step in the proofing process, after you've made sure all your other production elements are correct.

Continuous-tone and scanned RGB images must be converted to CMYK mode in order to create separations in your page-layout program (see Figure 7.17). Make sure that you've converted your scanned color images to CMYK format before exporting them as TIFFs from your image-editing software.

FIGURE 7.17 CMYK mode.

Be aware that in converting from RGB to CMYK, a color shift will occur. Bright colors that look great on your computer's monitor are harder to produce from process colors, causing muting in some areas of the spectrum.

In order for the high-resolution separations to be made in final production, you will need to further convert your CMYK TIFF files to DCS (Digital Color Separation) format. However, this step enlarges your CMYK TIFF file to four or five times its original size. It's a good idea to let your service bureau do this if you have limited storage.

T I P

If your page design calls for the graphic images to be rotated, stretched, or sheared, it's a good idea to perform those functions outside of the page-layout program to reduce the processing load on the imagesetter. Although technology and hardware capabilities have improved in recent years, a complex image rotated in the page-layout software can still slow processing down significantly. Your service bureau will surely thank you for considering their production schedule and bottom line profitability by making their work a little easier.

Step-by-Step Preparation

The most important things to watch when preparing your file for final output are fonts and pictures. If you make sure that the media you send to your service bureau include all of the fonts and pictures present in your page layout, you're more than halfway there.

Your biggest tool is communication with your service provider. They can help you avoid problems and save you unnecessary expense. If you spend a few moments beforehand asking for advice and discussing your requirements and expected results, you'll have fewer headaches and a better bottom line.

Here's a basic checklist to go over before submitting your files for output. Go over this with your service bureau and you should do just fine. The following checklist involves QuarkXPress.

1. After you've finished composing your document, select Picture Usage under the Utilities menu (see Figure 7.18).

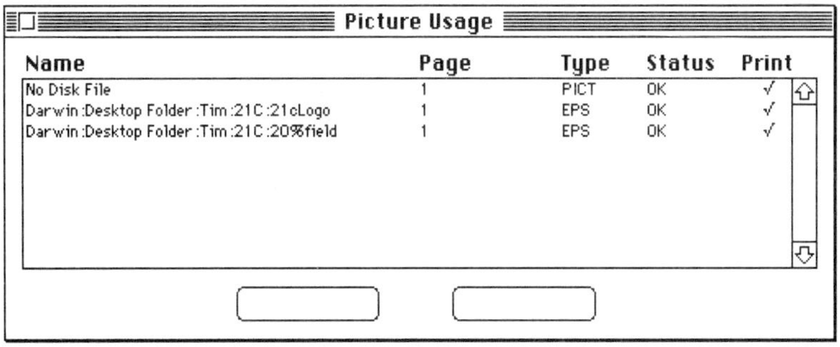

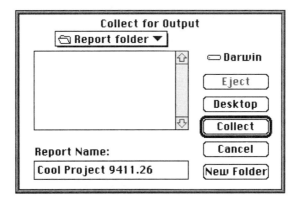

FIGURE 7.18 Picture usage.

This list will show you what images are present in your document, where they are, and if they are all current versions. This is a preliminary step that will help you determine if you need to do any last-minute image shuffling. The **Collect for Output** command will perform the final part of this process when you make your final copy for output. Replace or update any images if necessary.

2. Create a folder on your desktop and give it a name that includes the current date, like **projectname.10/21** (see Figure 7.19). This will help you identify it as the latest revision of your document.

FIGURE 7.19 Collect for output.

3. Now choose **Collect for Output** under the File menu (see Figure 7.20) and designate your newly created folder as the destination for all the files.

FIGURE 7.20 The new folder.

4. This is a big step. Close the current document and copy the folder containing the new copy and all the linked image files to the removable storage media that you'll use to transport the files to the service bureau.

5. Put the folder remaining on your drive in the trash (see Figure 7.21) and empty it.

FIGURE 7.21 Drag this into the trash, having made sure that the new copy is on your removable media.

6. Now open and print the QuarkXPress document again from your removable media. If there are any missing or updated imported image files, QuarkXPress will notify you automatically, asking if you want to update them now.

7. If there are any missing or updated files, you'll see them on your new proof and you'll be able to update and replace them as needed.

8. Repeat these steps again to make absolutely sure you have everything where it belongs.

The **Collect for Output** command also creates a text file listing all the images, colors, fonts, and attributes present in your document. Be sure to include this document as part of your order to the service bureau.

Most service bureaus will require you to submit a written work order with your service request. Filling out a preprinted order form is a good idea, if for no other reason than to have a paper record of your order for future reference in both locations. Even if you are sending your project over a modem, you should still consider sending a faxed copy of the work order as well.

Another benefit to filling out a written work order is that it will prompt you to make sure you have all the details of your project included. It may point out items you have overlooked.

These simple steps add a few minutes to your workload, but will surely save you (and your service bureau) headaches by avoiding the inconvenience and expense of a fumbled output.

Remember, QuarkXPress and other page-layout programs need to know where the original imported image exists in order to get the high-resolution information for accurate printing.

When you import a high-resolution grayscale, color, or EPS image into your page-layout program, you are actually only displaying a PICT preview of the image with a reference to the location of the high-resolution data, not the actual image. This is why it's crucial to include all your high-resolution images with your project when submitting for output.

If you forget to include an image and your service bureau doesn't catch the omission before imaging the job, the resulting image will print as a low-resolution bitmap on your final output.

Summary

Paper type, ink types, and production methods have a tangible impact on how you'll produce your electronic files. You can compensate for potential production errors using the software tools available on your system.

Talk with your service bureau about the project requirements and suggested production methods. The results of these discussions will help you plan a more efficient file and save the bureau time and effort while setting your images. Find out which type of prepress production is required for your job. Negatives might be overkill for a simple job.

Be sure to include all relevant images with your file. You'll avoid delays, phone calls, and potential re-runs.

Make sure your service bureau has all the fonts in the same format as the fonts present in your final document. Check with your font vendor about the rights conferred to you with the purchase of their fonts. It may or may not be legal to copy the fonts and include them with your project.

Check with your service bureau before submitting your work to make sure that they can meet your deadlines.

Make sure that any color separations are prepared correctly, with manual or automatic trapping values applied where appropriate. Remember, imported EPS graphics will not trap automatically without direct manual intervention in the program that created them. Make sure that all imported custom colors exist in the page-layout document before sending it off for imaging.

Continuous-tone color images require conversion to CMYK format before import to assure correct four-color separation. Color-matching software can't always offer totally accurate results on-screen. Be prepared for some differences, and get as many proofs as you can afford at every step in production.

The **Collect for Output** command in QuarkXPress's File menu works well and can help avoid headaches when making sure all imported high-resolution images are present in your final document.

Remember to talk with your service provider as much as you can to make sure you are providing all the files necessary to image your project correctly. You'll save yourself and your service bureau headaches and expense.

Certainly, there are plenty of opportunities for mistakes in this new and magical world of digital technology. We are working with complex tools these days, and we multiply the potential for errors when one or both parties don't fully understand the tools we are using.

Most prepress production problems can be averted before they cost you money if you're careful about proofing your work, communicating your needs and expectations from your service bureau, and proofing your work again before committing it to plates, ink, and a large printing press.

In the vast majority of responses to a query sent out to service bureaus nationwide, the one overriding desire among nearly all respondents was that clients communicate with their service bureaus.

Chapter 8

The Troubleshooter's Handy Guide to Common Problems and Solutions

Have you ever experienced mysterious problems with your computer system, like creating a file that wouldn't print? Or have you ever received that dreaded call from your service bureau, when not only did your job not print, but it crashed their imagesetter? Yikes! What to do? (See Figure 8.1.)

FIGURE 8.1 Yikes!

Most prepress production problems are easily solved and can be avoided with a few simple preventative measures. This chapter deals with some common production problems that you can avoid. Each example is illustrated and briefly explained with simple steps to help you avoid them in the future.

Time is cumulative. The time you save by avoiding a problem is time you can use at the end of the week to chase down new clients, take your existing clients out for coffee or cocktails, or just relax at home far away from keyboards, mice, and trackballs.

> Remember; the first step in solving a production problem is determining that you have one. If you check your files thoroughly before sending them to your service bureau and look for potential errors, you can avoid wasting time and resources in your production schedule. The trick, then, is in knowing where to look for errors.

Here's an easy checklist to help you avoid the most common production problems. Check the items on this list before you send your file out for imaging to save some headaches and avoid unpleasant surprises.

❋ Check your fonts. In QuarkXPress, make a list of all the fonts in your document using either the **Font Usage** command under the Utilities menu or by choosing **Collect for Output** under the File menu. Choosing **Collect for Output** creates a text file that lists all the pertinent information about the document (see Figures 8.2 and 8.3).

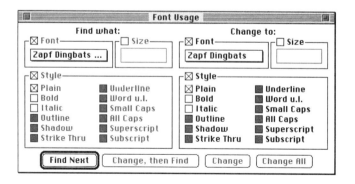

FIGURE 8.2 Font usage.

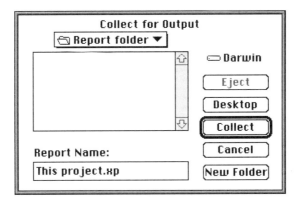

FIGURE 8.3 Collect for output.

* Check to see that all the images in your document are current. Choose **Picture Usage** under the Utilities menu to see that none of the images you've placed is missing or has been modified (see Figure 8.4).

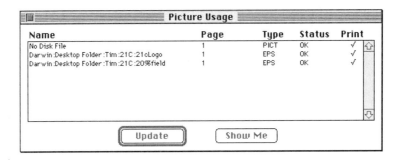

FIGURE 8.4 Picture usage.

* Choosing **Collect for Output** under the File menu will also check for missing or modified images and will make a copy of all high-resolution images in the selected folder.

* Make sure that all imported scans are of an appropriate file format and have been assigned the correct halftone screen values. Placed images that have not been assigned a screen value will use the document default values.

* Make sure that all colors defined in imported EPS documents are included in the QuarkXPress document's color palette. QuarkXPress 3.3 will automatically add colors present in the EPS document to the XPress document's colors palette, but sometimes even this can cause problems if there are too many colors and they are not all defined as process colors. QuarkXPress will print all the spot colors that are in a document on a separate plate, making for a potentially expensive and useless set of negatives.

* For correct separation, make sure that all your imported scanned color images have been converted to CMYK TIFF format.

* Print two copies of your laser proofs and submit one to the service bureau with your order. Print all the separations to your laser printer as well. Chances are that if there are any production problems present, they will show up at this stage. If they don't, you'll have a good reference copy from which to start your detective work in tracking down the source of your errors.

* Never, ever ask your service bureau to ship the negatives for your project directly to anyone without your first proofing the negatives with them. You'd be surprised at the sad stories and tales of woe that begin with a service bureau shipping unproofed negatives.

* Remember to discuss *in detail* the requirements and expectations you have for your project with your service bureau. The biggest benefit to this step is reviewing your project with an extra pair of eyes. Your service bureau will also be able to make recommendations as to the best production methods for your project.

* Make sure your production schedule includes enough time and expense to correct any problems that you don't catch at this stage of the game. The cost of one extra high-resolution color proof is pretty slim when compared to the cost of re-imaging an entire set of negatives or an entire press run.

Follow your checklist and you'll avert or avoid all of the problems that can be corrected on your end of the process. It's easy, and it will save you time, money, and most importantly, headaches.

Problems and Solutions

Here are some of the most common problems that can occur in desktop graphics production—and some simple solutions. Refer to this handy list whenever you're stumped by problem output. It's possible that your problems can be easily solved.

Problem 1

Your scanned halftones print as coarse bitmaps (see Figure 8.5). It is usually the case that the original imported image has been modified or is missing (see When you import an image to a page-layout program, what appears on the screen is actually a low-resolution PICT preview of the high-resolution information. Your page-layout program records the location of the actual image and draws the high-resolution image from that location when the image is being printed. This makes for smaller page-layout document sizes, but it makes you responsible for keeping track of all the placed images. If you change the location of a high-resolution image or modify it without updating it in your page-layout document, the application will look for the image and, not finding it, will print the low-resolution preview information that appears on your screen.

FIGURE 8.5 Bitmapped halftones.

Solution

Unfortunately, this is a fairly common problem that most service bureaus spend a good deal of time during the work week trying to resolve. You can avoid this problem every time by choosing the **Collect for Output** menu option under the File menu in QuarkXPress (see Figure 8.6).

FIGURE 8.6 Don't forget to collect your pictures.

Problem 2

After choosing **Update** for all your missing images, they have mysteriously repositioned themselves inconsistently throughout your document.

Solution

Once in a while, some imported images will reposition themselves within the picture box when updated. In the case of EPS files created in a PostScript drawing program such as Adobe Illustrator or Aldus Freehand, some changes can cause the image to create a new *bounding box* (the outside perimeter of the image area), which can cause the image to be repositioned. Your best bet for updating images without taking chances on repositioning is to click the **Show Me** button in the Picture Usage dialog box (see Figure 8.7) and watch it as you update the images individually. If there's a change from your original layout, you can correct it there or re-import the image.

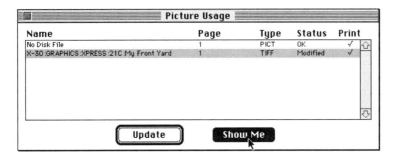

FIGURE 8.7 Show me.

Problem 3

Your scanned color image prints on the black plate only, or it prints as a grayscale halftone.

Solution

Remember, scanned color images must be converted to CMYK TIFF format in order to correctly separate in QuarkXPress. You can convert the scanned color image from RGB format to CMYK by using any of a number of image-conversion utilities, including the big gun, Adobe Photoshop.

If you're using Photoshop to convert your images, then you'll also have access to powerful editing and image correction tools. Read the how-to-do-it section on color correction for handy tips on getting the best possible output from your scans. First choose **CMYK** under the Mode menu, then choose **Save as...** under the File menu to choose a new image file format (see Figure 8.8).

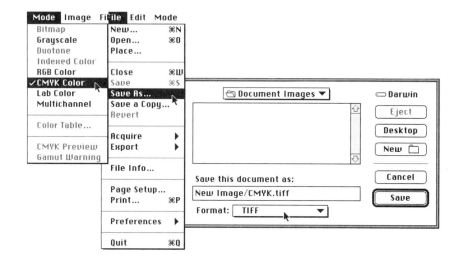

FIGURE 8.8 Save as...

You'll notice a slight shift in color balance with conversion to CMYK. Remember, you're trying to simulate a full 16.7 million different RGB colors using only four process colors. The same color-shift effect happens when converting a full-color photograph to process colors.

Problem 4

Color areas are not trapping correctly (see Figure 8.9).

FIGURE 8.9 Mis-registered colors.

Solution

If the object that isn't trapped correctly is a design element created in QuarkXPress, make sure that the trapping values have not been modified. First, check to see that the trapping value has not been changed in the Trap Specifications dialog box. Click **Edit Trap** in the Colors dialog box (see Figures 8.10 through 8.12).

FIGURE 8.10 the first step to checking traps is to choose the Colors... option under the Edit menu.

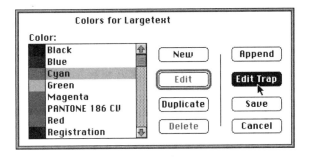

FIGURE 8.11 Next choose the color for which you want to check the trap and click the Edit Trap button.

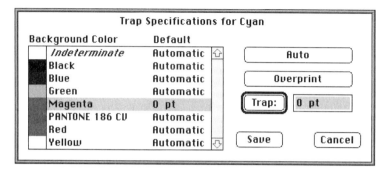

FIGURE 8.12 In this sample, one color's trapping relationship has inadvertently been changed to zero points, or no trap, for every instance where the selected color appears adjacent to Cyan. Where these two colors appear together, they will not trap— making it possible for inconsistencies on press to cause misregistration.

If the trapping values in the Trap Specifications dialog box are all correct, then you can check the Trap Info palette by choosing **Show Trap Info** under the View menu (see Figure 8.13. Select the object in question and check to see that the trap has not been adjusted for the individual object.

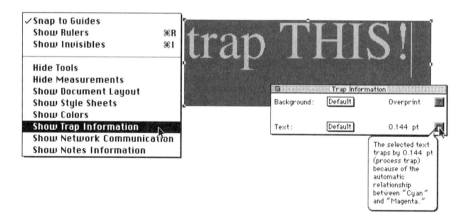

FIGURE 8.13 Trap information.

If the trapping problem is specific to an individual EPS graphic object, you should check to see that the proper steps to trap objects are taken in the program that created the art. Adobe Illustrator 5.5 now has a filter designed to automatically create traps for selected objects (see Figure 8.14).

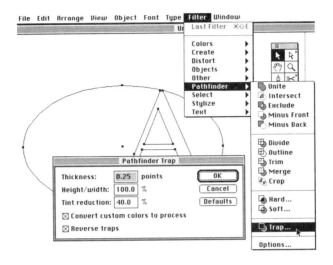

FIGURE 8.14 The Illustrator filter.

Problem 5

Duotones are not separating correctly in QuarkXPress (see Figure 8.15).

FIGURE 8.15 Incorrect duotone.

Solution

Creating a duotone from a scanned image in Adobe Photoshop is relatively easy. Simply create your duotone using two Pantone colors chosen from the Custom Colors palette in Photoshop, save the document as an EPS continuous tone image, and import it to QuarkXPress. Make sure that the colors chosen for the duotone effect in Photoshop are present in the QuarkXPress Colors palette. Simple enough?

In older versions of QuarkXPress, you had to choose, create, or name the color manually after importing the EPS duotone document. It was easy to overlook some characters in a color name like the *cv* or *u* that appears at the end of some Pantone colors, causing the page-layout program to incorrectly separate the colors. If you are not using the latest version of QuarkXPress, be sure to check the color names to make sure they are all spelled exactly the same.

The latest version of QuarkXPress now automatically adds the correct colors to the Colors palette as the image is imported to the XPress document (see Figures 8.16 through 8.18).

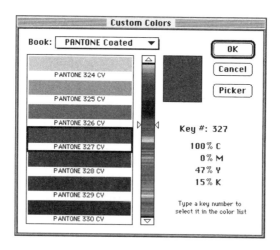

FIGURE 8.16 Selecting a PMS color for the duotone.

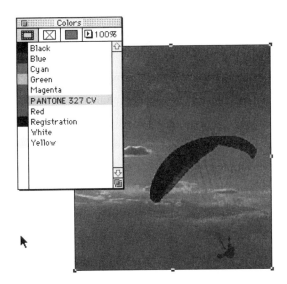

FIGURES 8.17 and 8.18 When imported to QuarkXPress, the colors are now automatically' added to the document's Colors palette.

Problem 6

Custom colors are printing on additional plates. This can cost you a few more dollars than expected when you order your final output, if you and your service bureau are not careful about proofing your work before ordering output. This problem can be caused by two simple errors that are easily overlooked in production.

Solution

If you are creating the new color in QuarkXPress and you forget to choose the **Process Separation** check box in the new Color Selection dialog box, the color will print as a spot color on its own plate. It is handy to create simple spot-color work using custom colors, but easy to overlook if you've added a handful of colors without checking the **Process Separation** check box.

This error can also occur in EPS artwork created in a PostScript drawing program. If you've created a complex illustration and made a lot of custom colors as you've gone along, you must remember to check the process-color option for each color in QuarkXPress after you've imported it (see Figures 8.19 and 8.20).

FIGURE 8.19 Your PostScript drawing program
allows you to specify custom colors in your artwork.

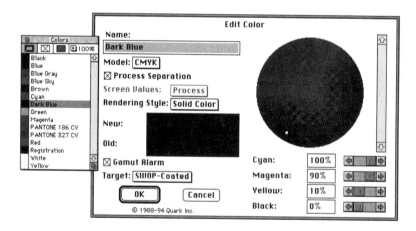

FIGURE 8.20 ...make sure the same color exists
in your page layout program for correct output.

Problem 7

Fonts display correctly but are substituted with Courier (or another non-specified font) in your high-resolution output (see Figure 8.21).

Looks like this...   Prints like this?

Understand that programmers live in a cold, dark world of mystery and imagination. Their sole mission being to generate miles and miles of code in short order, so the manufacturer can release their product only 12-18 months past their originally announced release date. Most programmers are kept in deep, dark, damp dungeons far beneath the deepest parking garage; intentionally separated from the rest of the world to prevent any normal human social contact that would possibly inhibit their code output.

Understand that programmers live in a cold, dark world of mystery and imagination. Their sole mission being to generate miles and miles of code in short order, so the manufacturer can release their product only 12-18 months past their originally announced release date. Most programmers are kept in deep, dark, damp dungeons far beneath the deepest parking garage; intentionally separated from the rest of the world to prevent any normal human social con-

FIGURE 8.21 Courier substitution.

Solution

This problem can be caused when the font you've specified in your page layout does not exist in your service bureau's system. The page-layout software automatically substitutes Courier (or another default typeface) for fonts that cannot be found in the system.

You can avoid this problem by making sure your service bureau is using the same version of the same font that exists in your document. Remember to supply a list of all fonts in your document by choosing **Collect for Output** under the File menu before transporting your job to the service bureau. The report this command generates will tell the service bureau which fonts are in use in your document.

Font substitutions can also be caused by conflicting font resource numbers. Each font you load into your system has a unique identifying font number assigned to it. With so many different font vendors in the world today, it's possible that identical font numbers may be generated by different manufacturers. If a font you've specified has the same identifying number as another font that already exists in your or your service bureau's system, a conflict can result, confusing your computer and causing font substitution.

There are reasonably priced third-party products available that resolve font-numbering conflicts. Suitcase II by Fifth Generation Systems is one of them. Not only does it help resolve font-numbering conflicts, it also serves as a convenient way to store and use specified groups of fonts that you can easily access and use your applications and loading the fonts into your system.

Problem 8

Fonts appear scrunched and overlapped, with varying output results (see Figure 8.22).

Nbof computer p
whithorough send
Hilgoodies that sl
pesprogram. Eas
that there is yet ur
you least expect it
programmers and

FIGURE 8.22 "Scrunched" fonts.

Solution

Make sure you've installed the correct and compatible versions of all your fonts in the system. This problem will usually show up when you have installed Adobe Type 1 fonts into the Fonts folder, where the TrueType version of the same font already exists. A big offender in this area is Times, for which both the TrueType and Type1 versions are named Times. The uninitiated user will not be aware of the format differences and may unknowingly install both families to a system (see Figure 8.23).

Times

Times

Times 12

FIGURE 8.23 Fixed fonts.

Most professionals prefer to exclude TrueType fonts from their systems for this and other reasons. Remember, the rendering and imaging capabilities of TrueType fonts are not always complementary. Service bureaus have an overwhelming preference for Type 1 fonts because of the inherent problems in imaging TrueType.

Problem 9

Fonts appear jagged at large sizes (see Figure 8.24).

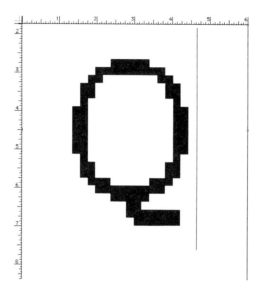

FIGURE 8.24 The font on the left is missing the appropriate printer font for correct rendering on screen. This font may or may not print correctly on your laser printer, depending on whether it is installed as part of the printer's ROM or downloaded to the printer's RAM.

Solution

The roots of this problem can be found in the method by which your computer renders fonts. If you are using Adobe Type 1 fonts in your production, you must install the accompanying printer (or outline) font with the screen font for each typeface you've installed in order for them to render correctly (see Figure 8.25).

Helvetica   Helve

FIGURE 8.25 Installing the screen font without the printer font in the Fonts folder will yield undesirable display and printed results.

Remember, TrueType fonts do not require a printer font for accurate on-screen rendering or printing; however, they are less efficient for high-resolution imaging.

This inefficiency can cause an entirely different set of problems for your service bureau. It's not uncommon for documents containing TrueType fonts to hang up an imagesetter with exceedingly long print times. Ask your service bureau what their experience has been with TrueType fonts, and whether they recommend using TrueType.

Problem 10

Graduated blends are banding. *Banding* is a term used to describe the effect of noticeable printed divisions between each shade of gray.

Solution

To correct for the banding effect, it helps to understand what causes it. High-resolution imagesetters are capable of producing only 256 different shades of gray. Some imaging devices will reproduce even fewer. The trick you have to learn is how to determine what will be the optimum number of steps in a graduated screen to create a seamless transition across a given distance.

The following is a simple demonstration of the concept of grayscale transitions (see Figures 8.26 through 8.291).

FIGURE 8.26 This bar shows an abrupt transition between black and white.

FIGURE 8.27 The same bar with the transition between black and white taking place using only for shades of gray. You can see clear divisions between each shade.

FIGURE 8.28 The transition between black and white becomes smoother with 16 shades of gray.

FIGURE 8.29 All 256 shades of gray make for a very smooth transition from black to white.

Banding is caused when there aren't enough shades available across a given distance (see Figure 8.30).

FIGURE 8.30 In this example, only 16 shades of gray are used across two bars of different length. The longer distance stretches the four shades of gray farther, making the divisions between shades more noticeable.

With a little math, you can calculate the optimum length for a graduated blend, the best number of blend steps, and the best halftone possible to render the graduation. Here's how to do it:

1. Determine the maximum number of gray shades possible on your printing device. To get this number, divide the maximum dot-per-inch resolution of the printing device by its optimum halftone screen ruling, and multiply it by itself. Thus, gray shades = $(dpi/lpi)^2$.

   For example, your 300-dot-per-inch laser printer will create a fairly reliable 54-line-per-inch halftone screen, so the equation for a 300-dpi laser printer would be: $(300 \text{ dpi}/54 \text{ lpi})^2 = 31$ shades of gray.

2. Now you can determine the best length for a blended object. Simply multiply the number of gray shades by 0.03 inch (Adobe recommends 0.03 inch, or 2.16 points as a small enough space to create an imperceptible blend). The equation is: number of gray shades multiplied by 0.03 inch = the optimum blend length.

The following are some examples (see Figures 8.31 through 8.33).

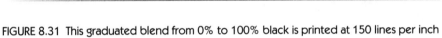

FIGURE 8.31 This graduated blend from 0% to 100% black is printed at 150 lines per inch on a high-resolution imagesetter capable of 3380 dots per inch (3380 dpi/150 lpi) 2 = (the maximum is 256 shades of gray). Two-hundred-fifty-six shades of gray times 0.03 inch = 7.7 inches as a maximum length for a perfect blend).

FIGURE 8.32 The blend that happens here is from 0% to 70% of black and is printed at 150 lpi. So the equation looks like this: 70% of 256 shades of gray is 179 shades of gray possible, multiplied by 0.03 inch = 5.3 inches as the maximum length with which you can make a smooth gradation.

FIGURE 8.33 This blend is a change of only 0% to 30%, but it is stretched across 5 inches of space, making the blend steps readily apparent.

T I P

You can also hide banding with coarse halftones or line screens. By creating a coarser halftone screen, a fewer-lines-per-inch screen frequency, you can effectively hide stepped transitions. Note that this is a low-tech solution to the problem, fitting nicely as an artistic effect whenever used (see Figure 8.34).

FIGURE 8.34 A coarser halftone.

Problem 11

A page full of imported EPS graphics is taking forever to print (see Figure 8.35).

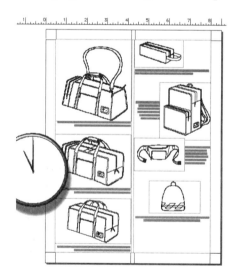

FIGURE 8.35 A complex page.

This problem shows up every now and again and starts out looking like an easy shortcut to the production artist. It happens when you import a complex EPS image and repeat it several times in a document with different parts of it showing in each picture box. You might think you're saving time, disk space, and effort by importing the same EPS image into several picture boxes (see Figures 8.36 through 8.38).

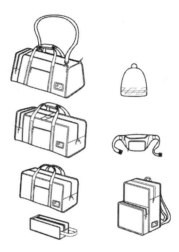

Figure 8.36 The offending image. It's supposed to print several times and in different orientations on the page.

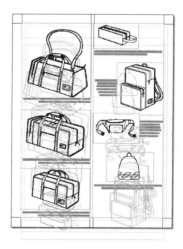

FIGURE 8.37 Parts of this image appear all over the page in different orientations and sizes.

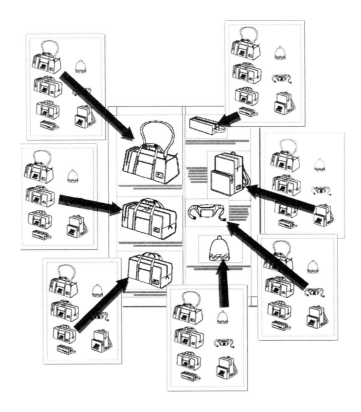

FIGURE 8.38 Here's what's happening to cause such long print times.
The Imagesetter must process the entire EPS image for each picture box
in this document, even though only part of each image actually shows up
on the page, thus creating a lot of unnecessary work for the imagesetter.

Solution

You can make the imagesetter's work much easier by creating a new EPS
image document for each object that is needed for the page-layout document
(see Figure 8.39).

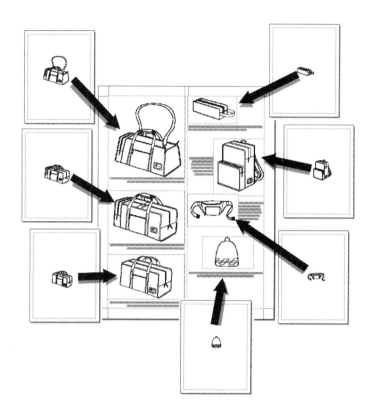

FIGURE 8.39 Create a new EPS document for each object in your
original document and import them individually to your QuarkXPress
page layout to make your imagesetter's processing job easier.

Just copy and paste each EPS object from the original into its own new EPS
document and re-import it into your page-layout document. This technique
does not significantly increase disk storage space requirements, but it greatly
reduces the amount of imagesetter processing time to create the high-resolution image.

Problem 12

Only part of the page prints. Your radical new newsletter design that your clients are going to love and approve (when they arrive in ten minutes) is only printing the top half of the page (see Figure 8.40). What to do? Don't panic. There are a few simple steps that you can take to remedy the situation.

FIGURE 8.40 This page only prints partially because there isn't enough printer memory to image the entire page.

The causes of this one are often memory-related. It was fairly common in some older third-party PostScript printers. Unless you've got some extra RAM laying around to install into your printer, you'll have to try simple adjustments and hope for the best.

Solution

Adjust the memory size of the PrintMonitor. If you're using System 7 or later, there's a system extension called PrintMonitor to control background document printing while you work in your applications in the foreground. You can change PrintMonitor's preferred memory size, then open your document and try to print it again. Most of the time this simple step will be all you need to resolve a low-memory printing problem (see Figures 8.41 and 8.42).

210

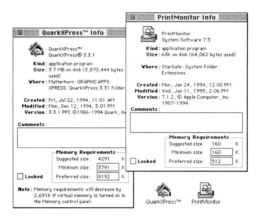

FIGURE 8.41 Change the memory settings for your applications, increasing the application memory size for the print monitor as well. The new preferred size is what the application will consume the next time you start your computer. See your Macintosh user's guide for more information on adjusting memory sizes and RAM management.

FIGURE 8.42 The complete printed document.

Next, adjust the memory size of your graphics application and reopen the application. Sometimes this is all you need to do to resolve a low-memory printing problem (see Figure 8.43).

In some cases, if you've opened and closed several applications over the course of the day, you can be working in a situation where your RAM has become so fragmented that your application could be having trouble spooling the document off to the background for printing. Save your changes and restart the computer. Surprisingly, this simple step will often clear up a fragmented RAM problem.

One great piece of advice that will take you places and help you solve many a problem: Always try the easiest, simplest, cheapest thing first. Then work your way up (and out) from there. Start by working with the system and memory resources immediately available to you in your computer. If this isn't enough to solve the problem, you can start looking around for other answers through third-party system utility software, and last but not least, your local Apple reseller or certified service technician can help as well.

Some problems can be solved by simply restarting your computer. If that doesn't work, try restarting with all your extensions disabled (Hold down the Shift key while the system is starting up—the "Welcome to Macintosh" screen will have a footnote saying, Extensions disabled). If the cause of your problems was conflicting INIT or CDEV extensions, you will be able to operate without them while you figure out which ones were causing the glitch. Be aware that this solution may disable some essential operating system software tools. System 7.5 ships with an extension/control panel device called Extension Manager to help solve this problem.

Many times these simple steps will be enough to clear up the problem. If they aren't, it may be time to review your system in a little more depth, looking at total system memory, potentially corrupted fonts, and conflicting extensions.

Problem 13

Unexpected end of file encountered message appears on screen. Uh-oh. This is a big one. Your file is history. A black hole is an adequate analogy to this condition. If you ever have nightmares about electronic prepress production, this one should be your scariest.

An unexpected end of file error happens when QuarkXPress crashes or is interrupted in the middle of trying to save a file. A file has a header that contains information about the file and the environment that existed when it was last saved, followed by all the data that the file contains, and finishes with a closing footer that identifies the end of the document and tells the program that the file is complete. If the file is truncated without this closing information, the application doesn't see the end of the file and can't complete the description of the file when it opens.

Solution

Make no mistake—this is an unrecoverable error. If you see this message, your file is completely lost. You will not be able to recover any part of it. It's gone. Sorry! The best you can hope for is that you had the presence of mind to enable the Auto-Backup feature sometime before this happened (see Figure 8.43).

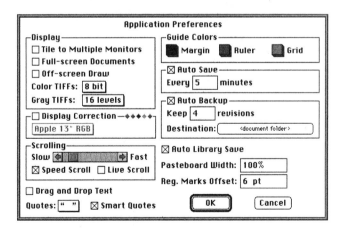

FIGURE 8.43 Note the auto save interval is set to five minutes
in this example. If the program crashes, only five minutes' work
will be lost and the four previous versions will be available as a backup.

There's an old hang-gliding axiom that states, "Never fly any higher than you're willing to fall." The same wisdom applies to choosing a time interval between auto-saves and auto-backups. Save only as often as you can afford to lose your work. If you can afford to lose an hour's work, set your autosave auto backup interval to one hour. Keep in mind that in a shop as busy as yours, minutes count.

Once again, that ounce of prevention will save you untold hours of reconstructing complex documents lost to the dreaded Unexpected end of file demons.

Problem 14

Color PostScript illustrations separate without trapping. Aha! This one will catch up with you sooner or later, if it hasn't already. Misregistration has been known to sneak up on unsuspecting new initiates to the art of color-printing production (see Figure 8.44).

FIGURE 8.44

Because PostScript illustrations are objects defined in a drawing program, there is no way to adjust the objects outside of the drawing software. There are two remedies to this problem. One will help you avoid it, and the other will help you correct it.

Solution

To avoid this problem, you can create mechanical traps in the PostScript drawing software that creates your artwork. Manually, this can be accomplished by specifying a stroke around a shape, with the same color as the interior of the shape. In addition, Adobe Illustrator 5.5 has a new filter that lets you assign overprinting areas to act as traps for your separated colors (see Figures 8.45 and 8.46). Larger, more complex pages will require a higher order of intervention; the Scitex DolevPS2 or other software-based auto-trapping utility.

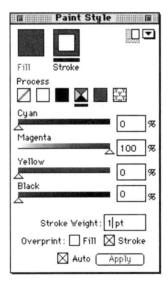

FIGURE 8.45 The trapping information in Illustrator.

FIGURE 8.46 The corrected image.

Problem 15

TIFF/PICT/EPS images are printing at low resolution. A picture is worth a thousand words, many of them expletives if your images end up bitmapped in your final output (see Figure 8.47).

FIGURE 8.47 This photo was supposed to print like this, but turns out like this... What happened?

This used to happen more often than it does now, but the causes are the same. The big difference between then and now is that in the past, when an application didn't find the high-resolution TIFF image, it just beeped— without any clue as to the problem. Of course, today, the application will alert you to missing or modified TIFF images—*if* you've specified that requirement in the application's Preferences dialog box (see Figure 8.48).

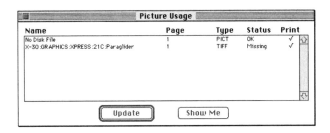

FIGURE 8.48 The Picture Usage dialog box.

Solution

To paraphrase an old anecdote: an ounce of prevention is a lot easier to swallow than the delivery charges to send missing TIFF files to your service bureau. There are two simple ways to prevent this. First, enable the **Auto Picture Import** option in the General Preferences dialog box in QuarkXPress to alert you to missing or modified high-resolution images. Second, use the **Collect for Output** command under the File menu prior to sending your files to the service bureau. This will copy all high-resolution TIFF, PICT, and EPS images to the destination folder prior to sending your media to the service bureau or printer (see Figure 8.49).

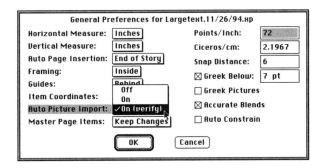

FIGURE 8.49 You can tell QuarkXPress to alert you if any high-resolution images in your document are missig or modified.

What the Professionals Say

Part of the research undertaken for this book involved an extensive survey of service bureaus and printers nationwide, to elicit their opinions and experiences with various problems and techniques in the electronic prepress production world. This helped provide some real-world insight by the people who face every imaginable problem every day. From user-related skills and technique problems to software and compatibility trouble to hardware and everything in between, these people had the most to say about what works and what doesn't.

Their experiences with the various hardware and software products as well as the publishers of these products is an invaluable resource to everyone in this industry. By all means, before purchasing any product, consult with the people who use it every day for a real-world evaluation of whether it lives up to its advertised claims.

The following is a summary of their responses to questions about their preferences and opinions on the state of the business and the tools we use in it.

The survey was designed to expose opinions and experiences with specific business practices and software products. Overall, there were surprising preferences for specific software products over others, indicating a desire to move toward better standards in file formats, applications, and business practices. It was encouraging to see how many service bureaus actually held their clients' success as a core value to their business. The sharing of advice, information, and helpful hints was common to almost all respondents as a basic business premise.

Feature wars continue to escalate between software products. While user attraction to products is based on such features, 'there was an overwhelming preference among service bureau operators for products that proved most reliable when it came to output problems. The real test of a product is not in the pretty pictures it displays on your screen, but in how accurately it creates a precise image on the film that makes the plates. In every case, they recommended QuarkXPress over PageMaker, Adobe Illustrator over FreeHand, Adobe Type 1 fonts over TrueType, and Macintosh over Windows. You can call them.

The 80/20 Rule

Service bureau operators also expressed an interesting postulation called the 80/20 rule, which presents that 80% of the projects entering the service bureau's workflow will ultimately take up 20% of the available time during the week, while 20% of the projects that come in the door will consume 80% of their time to complete. The lesson? Try to be part of the 80% that doesn't consume your service bureau's resources. Be a better-educated client and a more efficient production artist.

Some Advice from Service Bureaus

Proof, proof, and proof again—as often as you can, in every step of the production process. Even your basic run-of-the-mill laser proofs are good enough, and remember to print proofs of all your separations on your laser printer as well.

View service bureau operators as your partners in the business. It's in their best interests that you get their best service. They are not your adversaries. Trust their advice.

Chapter 9

Legal Issues

* ❋ Who's responsible for what
* ❋ Other legal issues

What Happens When There's a Problem

What do you do if after all your work and careful proofing, there's a problem in the final printing? Who's at fault? Who's responsible for the changes, corrections, or (shudder) the reprinting?

As mentioned previously, most problems can be averted if you take a few simple steps, such as getting an accurate proof every step of the way. Current technology being the way it is, unexpected results are bound to pop up from time to time. It's a good idea to know where your responsibilities and liabilities begin and end when dealing with service bureaus.

Fault is difficult to assign when there are problems with a file. Unfortunately, *fault* is a word we apply when looking for someone else to pay for a mistake. Is it your fault if a halftone screens at an unintended resolution? Is it the service bureau's fault for imaging it incorrectly (provided that you've specified that line screen in your instructions)? Is it the software manufacturer's fault if the software produces an unexpected result where no value is assigned?

Suppose you have submitted a file to be imaged at your service bureau and have supplied a comprehensive set of proofs with your request. Somehow, some of the fonts have been substituted by the default font. Did you supply a list of all fonts present in the document? Did they check to see that all of the specified fonts are present in their system? Are the fonts all current versions made by the same manufacturer? Who pays for the miles of now-useless film when this occurs?

Who pays for these mistakes depends largely on the relationship you have with your service bureau. If you regard each other as partners, equally responsible for each other's success in your projects, then an amicable resolution is easy to accomplish. Most service bureaus interviewed for this book responded that output problems are often written off as experience, and expenses incurred may be split with the client—up to a certain point. These problems are a lot easier to swallow if both parties are aware of potential problems and have taken appropriate precautions along the way, such as printing and submitting accurate proofs with the job. When there's a problem, even simple laser proofs give everyone a reference copy to compare with unexpected output.

CYA: Cover Your Assets

Printing and keeping an auditable trail of proofs for every step in the production process will go a long way toward avoiding problems and misunderstandings later on down the line. Unpleasant finger-pointing can result in damaged client/supplier relationships. Work into your schedule and budget enough time and expense to create proofs and correct potential errors at every step in production.

Problems that turn up late in the production process tend to be the most costly. Reprinting a job or even holding the presses while you mechanically strip corrections in are the stuff of every production artist's nightmares. It makes sense to avoid these problems whenever possible.

Copyright Law

Who really owns your work? Is it really that important in this age of instantly reproducible artwork? Is your work protected if you prominently placed standard copyright or registration symbols? What exactly is copyright protection?

Any kind of artwork—an illustration, diagram, or logo symbol—is protected by U.S. law against someone else using your artwork without your permission. Your work is automatically protected against unauthorized use without your intervention. However, it's a good idea to signify your intention to protect your work by indicating a © symbol and the date of creation.

U.S. law also protects the expression of ideas, but not the ideas themselves. For example, the concept of a box at the end of your driveway into which mail is delivered by the United States Postal Service (a mailbox) cannot be copyrighted. However, a bright periwinkle blue neon-rimmed propeller-driven container in the shape of a hamburger can be protected as an expression of the mailbox idea.

Current laws, as they are written, make a distinction between *work for hire*—in which an artist produces original artwork as immediately directed by an employer, at the employer's location, using the employer's equipment—and *original artwork*—created for a specific purpose by freelance artists at their own location, using their own tools, with the art then being sold to an employer for a specified price. Copyrights on artwork falling under the definition of work for hire belongs to the employer, to be used at the employer's discretion.

Copyrights for work created for resale to an employer (assuming you are a freelancer, that is, a self-employed entity) remain yours to dispose of as you see fit. Make sure that you're aware of any copyrights that you assign as part of any creative project. They are a valuable commodity, the rights to which are negotiable at your discretion.

A great contact for artists' rights and responsibilities is the Graphic Artist's Guild of America. They serve as a lightening rod for the graphic arts industry and can offer valuable advice and ethical guidelines. Every major metropolitan area supports a chapter. Check your phone book for the one nearest you.

Using Photography

With so much work being done with scanners, stock photography, and clip art these days, how do you know what you can use and what requires a release? Generally, the basic rule is that anyone who is recognizable as an individual must give you their consent to have their likeness reproduced in print. The same applies to digital video and sound reproduction. It's a good idea to obtain a model release from anyone whose image you use in a publication.

The same rules that apply to a piece of artwork also apply to photography. You cannot use the work of another individual or entity (no matter how incomplete) without his or her permission. This even applies to portions of an image that have been heavily manipulated. Flipped, flopped, reversed, or distorted—if the work is recognizable (especially by the original copyright holder), you are taking the chance of incurring legal penalties for unlawful use and possible copyright violation. The basic rule of thumb to follow is: Always obtain permission to use anything that you did not create.

Registering Copyrights

It is commonly believed that every original work created by an artist is automatically protected by copyright law. Enforcing this protection is not always practical. For a small fee, you can register your copyright with the appropriate federal agencies, further protecting your work against unauthorized use or reproduction. Depending on the volume of the work you do, this may not always be practical. It's a definite judgment call as to whether it's worth the effort of registering with the federal government. Contact your local copyright attorney for the straight scoop on protection of intellectual property.

The Birth Of Stock—Everything on CD-ROM

Given the potential for litigation in copyright disputes, as well as the sudden downturn in the photography and illustration markets when computers came into popular use, it is now possible to purchase entire collections of high-resolution graphics and photographic images on CD-ROM. CDs hold hundreds of megabytes of information, making them an excellent archiving and distribution medium for graphics and photography. Most CD collections are available for a flat price that includes a copyright license to use for any purpose. As always, make sure that license for unlimited use is included before committing anything to print. It's a good idea to contact the publisher of the media to confirm this with each use or purchase.

Software Licenses

Who owns your software? You might be surprised to find out that in most cases, you do not! If you've never taken a close look at the license agreement that shipped with your software, take a look at it now. It makes for good reading and a nervous chuckle. Imagine putting out good money (and a lot of it) for a product, all the time knowing that even after money has changed hands, the product you've purchased still belongs to the person to whom you just gave the money.

That's right. Not only can the software company tell you how and where your (their) product can be used, but at their sole discretion, they can retrieve your (their) software from you for noncompliance with the rules set forth in the license agreement. On top of all this, the software manufacturer specifically disclaims any warranty or guarantee that the product will even work on your machine.

Imagine that. What a country. As crazy as all that sounds, there's some logic in the intent of all these regulations and disclaimers. Naturally, they have to cover their assets against any unforeseen litigation from disappointed customers, who may be using computers and configurations of which nobody else has ever heard. More importantly, they have to protect themselves against ne'er-do-wells who may purchase, copy, and illegally resell the software, thereby robbing the company of potential income. Without these protections, they might just as well give away the farm, bankrupt their investors, and drive themselves right out of business.

You are, in fact, purchasing from the software manufacturer the right to use their software in a certain way, for as long as you want, with the option of purchasing upgrades as they become available. Ownership of the product (in most cases) remains with the publisher or manufacturer. It's a complex web of legalese and license regulations, but the object is to protect the intellectual property of the people who create these remarkable products.

Font Licenses

The use of digital fonts and font software has unraveled a whole new ball of twine in the industry and has been the target of policy and license changes recently. Currently, the official word from Adobe on the use of their fonts is that it is illegal to transport copies of their fonts to your service bureau for imaging.

Adobe has moved from a printer-based licensing scheme to a CPU-based licensing scheme to ensure fair and reasonable compensation for their product. In purchasing an Adobe font, you are licensed to use it on up to five different computers connected to a single PostScript printing device.

The Bottom Line on Fonts

If you've created a document that uses Adobe fonts not already owned by the service bureau or printing establishment, they must purchase the font from Adobe to image the project. Luckily, service bureaus are privy to some very preferential pricing on fonts as an encouragement to use Adobe products.

There is one possible way to get around this, in order to send files to a printer who may not own a particular font. You can create a PostScript file with the font embedded in the document, in effect a picture of the document, known as a PostScript *dump*. Adobe doesn't see this as infringement because it doesn't allow access by the receiving party to the font itself. Of course, the caveat to this is that a PostScript dump makes it impossible to make even minor changes to a page once it's been converted to a PostScript file.

If you are using typefaces published by other vendors, be sure to check their usage licenses and policies before distributing them with your work. Some may differ from the standard practices in the industry.

Summary

Who's responsible for errors in production? This is such a sticky issue that it cannot be answered without building a complete scenario for every possible occurrence. The best you can do is to follow the production process very carefully, proof your work at every possible step, and save an auditable trail of proofs. This should help if a disagreement arises. Make open communication between you and your service bureau a priority. Treat and respect your service bureau as a partner in your business endeavors.

Copyrights and licenses make up the legal blanket protecting the creators of many products, from artwork to software, against unlawful exploitation of their intellectual property. Copyrights protect you against someone purloining your artwork and using it to their profit without your permission. Software licenses protect manufacturers from the same crime.

Different software manufacturers provide and enforce the license for the use of their products in different manners. You can be a better and more informed customer (while protecting yourself against becoming an unknowing criminal) by being aware of the usage license granted with the purchase of software products.

It's a serious issue. Businesses have been lost, persons have been prosecuted, and criminal sentences have been passed over software license and copyright violation. Take the time to become informed.

Chapter 10

Don't Let This Happen to You

Almost everyone you meet in this industry will have a great job-from-hell story to relate to you about that one unprintable project that drove them nuts getting produced. Here are a few of those stories as they have been related over the course of several lunches. Although none can be directly substantiated or corroborated due to their embarrassing natures, they are all professed to be true stories—and a pertinent lesson from which we can all learn.

Horror Stories

Macintosh history is filled with great humorous anecdotes about well-intentioned but not very knowledgeable users trying to solve their everyday production problems with solutions that might make perfect sense to the uninitiated. One common tale relates the story of a hapless computer user who was having trouble printing a file. After several attempts, the friendly local service bureau operator asked its client to send in a copy of the disk with the problem file on it.

The next day, the service bureau's overnight delivery service arrived with an envelope package marked *rush*. Inside the envelope was a photocopy of the disk (both sides) made by laying the disk on the copy machine.

One service bureau offers this advice about fonts: Just as you should never play cards for money with a guy whose first name is the same as a major U.S. city, you should also never use a font whose name is the same as a city.

Another great don't-let-this-happen-to-you story is the one about a one-person design shop who dropped off his very important final digital project at his service bureau on a high-density cartridge—and then left for an extended vacation. The designer was scheduled to be gone for a few weeks somewhere in the backwoods, far from telephones, while his diligent service bureau imaged his job and delivered it to the printer. Wouldn't you know it—one image file was missing from one page, preventing the job from imaging.

The service bureau did finally hear from the designer by telephone a week later. Shocked at the omission, he sent a friend to retrieve a copy of the file at the designer's residence, not far from the service bureau. Unfortunately, the friend sent on this crucial errand was not familiar with computers, files, desktop publishing, or printing (or even electricity, it seemed).

The designer described to the friend what a disk looked like and where to deliver it, only to find that the service bureau lacked the necessary device drivers to read the disk. The clock was ticking. The deadline neared. After scrambling to secure a device driver to read the disk, it was found that the black plate was missing from the DCS file.

All ended happily, though. The service bureau was able to locate the source photo and re-scan it for the designer, who returned from vacation to a great printed piece and a happy and relieved (but nervous) client.

If these stories do nothing else, they should re-emphasize the value of a current set of proofs and careful attention to and partnership with your service bureau operator. Remember to proof your work every step of the way. Print the separations on your laser printer. Be kind to your service bureau. They are your friends.

Easter Eggs

No discussion of computer products is complete without a thorough send-up of Easter eggs; those little hidden goodies that show up in unexpected places in a program. Easter eggs are a sure sign that there is yet untapped creativity where you least expect it—inside the heads of bored programmers and code warriors.

It is commonly held that programmers live in a cold dark world of mystery and imagination. Their sole mission is to generate miles and miles of code in short order, so the manufacturer can release their product only 12 to 18 months past the originally announced release date. Most programmers are kept in deep, dark, damp dungeons, far beneath the deepest parking garage, intentionally separated from the rest of the world to prevent any normal human social contact that would possibly inhibit their code output.

According to popular myth, living in the darkness as they do, eating the most vile of junk foods, and drinking only high-caffeine soft drinks, programmers have evolved into a unique humanoid species unto them-selves with no social skills for and no desire to live among the general population. (There was once talk of developing a programmer petting zoo where children would be allowed to wander among them and see them perform simple tricks for bits of pork rinds and cheese crisps, but the plan was immediately canceled after the project's promoters actually met a programmer in the flesh. Frightened and astonished, they discontin-ued any further market research.)

In spite of all that is said about them, in spite of all the rumors and innuendos, and in part because of their high caffeine intake, programmers have retained a remarkably dry sense of humor throughout their recent evolution. This is evidenced by the existence of Easter eggs in many soft-ware products.

One of the great things about Easter eggs is that programmers rarely reveal the fruits of their sarcastic humor to the marketing or technical support departments, waiting instead until the technical support staff starts getting inane phone calls from disturbed users proclaiming that their new software is doing weird things. QuarkXPress and Adobe Illustrator both have world-class Easter eggs that you can find with a little effort.

Without revealing the full results of these Easter egg hunts, here are the steps to finding them yourself. While using QuarkXPress, choose the QuarkXPress Environment dialog box by holding down the **Shift** key while you choose **About QuarkXPress** under the Apple menu. (You can also hold down the **Option** key while you press the **Help** button on your extended keyboard.) Then hold down the **Shift, Option,** and **Command** keys while you click in the center of this dialog box. Hah!

Here's another favorite QuarkXPress Easter egg: Everyone knows the keyboard shortcut for deleting an item in the program; hold down the **Command** and **K** keys. Now try that while also holding down the **Option** key with the same keyboard shortcut. Hah! (See Figure 10.1.)

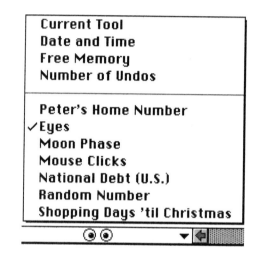

FIGURE 10.1 Where did this guy come from?

Adobe Illustrator has a grand Easter egg that will delight and amuse you and provide hours of endless fun and entertainment. You'll notice the information field at the bottom-left corner of the Illustrator window. You can change the information that appears there by holding down the mouse button while the cursor is over it, displaying a pop-up menu showing other information display options. Here's the trick: Try the same operation while holding down the **Option** key. Hah! Hah!

Ever wonder who the ROM wonks and PowerPC geeks are for Adobe Illustrator? Choose **About Illustrator** under the Apple menu and wait 15 seconds. The answer will come to you (see Figure 10.2).

FIGURE 10.2 Illustrator's creators.

Do you want to know who Adobe's favorite customer is? Choose **About Photoshop** under the Apple menu and watch as the credits scroll just like the movies. You'll see the name of Adobe's favorite customer. Try choosing **About Photoshop** under the Apple menu while you hold down the **Command** key. But wait, there's more! After the credits scroll the entire list, wait and watch for some special messages that appear just for their favorite and most patient customers. Now try holding down the **Option** key and clicking on the **Adobe logo** at the top-left corner of the window (see Figure 10.3).

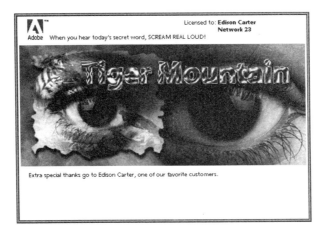

FIGURE 10.3 Adobe's favorite customers.

233

It's clear that the true value added to software upgrades is not in enhanced feature sets, but in the inclusion of humorous Easter eggs. Call your favorite software publisher today and demand more Easter eggs. Be the life of any party (or propeller-head user-group meeting). Amaze your friends and impress your family by showing off your knowledge of secret Easter eggs in your favorite software products.

Index

Q

R

U

V

W

X

Y

About the CD

CD-ROMs are a wonder of today's technology. Just a few years ago, this book would have been packaged without a disk or with a single 3.5" diskette containing a few tools to help your work. Now, we can package the equivalent of over a hundred of those same diskettes (which alone would have cost more than twice the cover price of this book) into the space that a single diskette would occupy.

What's on the CD

There are several folders and a file on the CD-ROM enclosed with the book. The single file is left in the root directory to enable the Hypercard Video Tour to run from the CD-ROM. The individual folders contain some things that hopefully will make your desktop prepress experiences easier.

The Video Tour

This is the most computer-intensive part of the entire CD-ROM. It was written for 8-bit color Macs with 8 megabytes of RAM running System 7.01 or higher. If you don't have these specifications, the video tour may not run, but give it a try anyway. It has worked perfectly on machines with monochrome monitors and considerably less memory.

There's over 100 megabytes of digital video footage on the CD-ROM detailing two of the most arcane parts of the printing process—a prepress service bureau and a printing plant. Hopefully, after viewing the footage, you'll have a better idea of some of the topics discussed in the book and some sympathy for your service bureau when they tell you your film is going to take another few hours to output.

The digital movies in this application require the QuickTime extension in order to run. You must install this extension before running the application program. If it isn't installed properly, the movies will not run at all on your machine.

If you already have the QuickTime Extension installed on your Macintosh, you can skip the following instructions and launch the tour by double-clicking the Interactive Tour icon.

1. Copy the QuickTime Extension into your Macintosh System Folder by dragging it onto the System Folder icon. System 7 will alert you to its intention of placing it into the Extensions folder where it belongs.

    If you are using a PowerMacintosh you'll need to drag the QuickTime PowerPlug extension to the same place with the QuickTime Extension.

2. Re-start your Macintosh to complete the installation process. As the computer is starting up, you'll see the QuickTime extension displayed briefly near the bottom of your computer's monitor.

Now you can double-click on the Interactive Tour icon to launch it and run the program.

Notes About the Program Itself:

1. This tour was created using HyperCard and QuickTime movies, then converted into a stand-alone application—you don't need HyperCard in order to use this stack.

2. This application will run on any (68030 or later) Macintosh computer that is running System 7 or later.

3. For best operation you'll need at least 3 megabytes of free RAM available to run this stack. Moving the application to your hard drive and increasing the RAM requirements is not recommended because the application will then ask you for each movie title before playing it from the CD-ROM.

4. While HyperCard is a relatively universal application for distribution of data like this, it has its drawbacks when it comes to displaying color. Expect this application to run a little slow at times. The places where the speed deficit is most noticeable are:

   ❋ at startup—it may seem to take a while for the application to get started. There are a few non-native resources at work to make this application colorful and interesting.

   ❋ while running—travelling from card to card (or movie to movie) you may see a second or so delay between cards depending on what class of Macintosh you are using. You will likely see a few seconds delay when travelling between backgrounds.

   ❋ when quitting—the application stops and thinks for a moment before closing.

Hypercard Helpers

Hypercard Helpers contains a number of self-running Hypercard stacks that will hopefully assist you in ways too numerous to mention. There's a stack to calculate blends, a stack to write up invoices, a stack of Quark 3.3 keyboard shortcuts, a dpi/lpi calculator, and many more. There are even a few demos of what Hypercard can do for you in the "Fun Stacks!".

About Using These Stacks

It's a good idea to copy this entire folder to your hard disk for temporary/permanent storage. The entire folder will occupy about 2.5M of space on your hard drive and will require about 2M of free RAM (a generous estimate) to run quickly and smoothly.

What's Included Here?

In this folder you'll find the HyperCard 2.2 Player application that will allow you to view and operate these stacks regardless of whether you already have HyperCard on your system. (All Macintosh systems ship with HyperCard Player installed.) The player will allow you to work with the stacks, but will not allow you to alter their scripts for customization. To do this you'll need to contact Claris Corporation and secure a copy of the HyperCard Developer's Kit which includes a full-blown copy of the application and plenty of development tools.

If you already own a fully operational HyperCard, copy everything EXCEPT the HyperCard player to your hard drive. These stacks will preferentially open the HyperCard player on startup. If you have an older version of the HyperCard Player, you may want to consider replacing it with the 2.2 version supplied here.

Why Copy to the Hard Drive?

The entire folder will consume about 2.5M of hard disk space. You may eventually want to discard some of the "fun" stacks after you've tried them, making the disk space requirements smaller, but overall, 2.5M is not a large commitment.

Some of the stacks are designed to create additional text files that you'll want to copy and use. Since CD-ROM technology doesn't allow you to change the contents of the CD-ROM disk, you'll receive an error message if you try to run some of these stacks from the CD.

How to Use the Stacks

Each of the stacks perform a simple but useful productivity-enhancing function. To use them, simply double-click to launch the stack. Each stack has instructions and help text that will appear as you open the stack.

Art Collection

Art Collection contains a whole library of digital images that you can use in your own work for anything you can imagine. Most of the images are in EPS, TIFF, or Photoshop format to ease your use of them. You'll find backgrounds, clip art, and Photoshop textures and objects ready for you to play with.

Digital PMS Color Tables

This document was created as a sample to test the color fidelity of a variety of color printing mediums. To use this file:

Print the documents from both QuarkXPress and Adobe Illustrator.

Print the documents on a variety of color printing devices such as:

* color inkjet printer
* color thermal wax transfer printer
* color dye sublimation proof
* four-color process matchprint or chromalin

Then compare each output medium to each other to see where colors shift.

Compare the colors the video display of the colors (the RGB representation) on your computer's monitor. Compare the printed colors against your handy Pantone color swatch book samples.

This will give you an idea of how colors will print differently from one color proofing device to another, as well as give your printer a simple to produce guide to ink color fidelity.